About This Book

Why is this topic important?

Organizations are faced with market challenges caused by shorter product life cycles, increased competition, and investor demand to run lean, cost-effective operations. Consequently, organizations must differentiate themselves through their ability to out-invent, out-think, and out-execute the competition. When asked, most CEOs say the greatest challenge they face is finding the skilled talent they need to be competitive. This increasing need for skilled and knowledgeable people to deal with a complex and constantly changing world has led to a proliferation of corporate universities. The corporate university is the vehicle for turning your organization into one that is constantly learning and that is developing creative people capable of adapting to rapid changes and delivering business results. It should be a hub for the exchange of ideas, for guiding both formal and informal learning, and for experimenting with ways to help people learn more and learn it faster. Developing an effective corporate university is critical to solving the talent and competitive problems facing organizations today.

What can you achieve with this book?

This book will guide you step-by-step through the process of designing, developing, and executing your corporate university. With this book, you will get a head start on your competitors because you will have the cutting-edge ideas, illustrated with examples of both best practices and problematic scenarios. By using this book and following through chapter by chapter, you will end up with a corporate university that is well thought out, has upper management understanding and support, is properly funded to achieve its goals, and is able to measure its success.

How is this book organized?

This is intended as a workbook. Everyone involved in creating the corporate university should have a copy and it should be marked up, written in, and used for group discussions. The chapters are laid out in an order that has been used in the development of many successful corporate universities. It starts by helping articulate the reasons for creating a corporate university and follows step-by-step through the choices of a strategic orientation, the development of a governance structure, and the formalizing of an organization structure. Subsequent chapters discuss budgeting and funding, how to staff the corporate university, and how to develop and deliver curriculums in a variety of formal and informal ways. The final chapters discuss how to market the corporate university and how to measure its success.

About Pfeiffer

Pfeiffer serves the professional development and hands-on resource needs of training and human resource practitioners and gives them products to do their jobs better. We deliver proven ideas and solutions from experts in HR development and HR management, and we offer effective and customizable tools to improve workplace performance. From novice to seasoned professional, Pfeiffer is the source you can trust to make yourself and your organization more successful.

Essential Knowledge Pfeiffer produces insightful, practical, and comprehensive materials on topics that matter the most to training and HR professionals. Our Essential Knowledge resources translate the expertise of seasoned professionals into practical, how-to guidance on critical workplace issues and problems. These resources are supported by case studies, worksheets, and job aids and are frequently supplemented with CD-ROMs, websites, and other means of making the content easier to read, understand, and use.

Essential Tools Pfeiffer's Essential Tools resources save time and expense by offering proven, ready-to-use materials—including exercises, activities, games, instruments, and assessments—for use during a training or team-learning event. These resources are frequently offered in looseleaf or CD-ROM format to facilitate copying and customization of the material.

Pfeiffer also recognizes the remarkable power of new technologies in expanding the reach and effectiveness of training. While e-hype has often created whizbang solutions in search of a problem, we are dedicated to bringing convenience and enhancements to proven training solutions. All our e-tools comply with rigorous functionality standards. The most appropriate technology wrapped around essential content yields the perfect solution for today's on-the-go trainers and human resource professionals.

Pfeiffer
www.pfeiffer.com

Essential resources for training and HR professionals

The Corporate University Workbook

Launching the 21st Century

Learning Organization

Kevin Wheeler

in collaboration with

Eileen Clegg

Pfeiffer

A Wiley Imprint

www.pfeiffer.com

Published by Pfeiffer
An Imprint of Wiley
989 Market Street, San Francisco, CA 94103-1741   www.pfeiffer.com

ISBN: 0-7879-7339-4

Acquiring Editor: Lisa Shannon	Manufacturing Supervisor: Bill Matherly
Director of Development: Kathleen Dolan Davies	Editorial Assistant: Laura Reizman
Developmental Editor: Susan Rachmeler	Template Design: Eileen Clegg
Production Editor: Nina Kreiden	Graphics: Mary J. Gillot
Editor: Suzanne Copenhagen	

Printed in the United States of America

Printing   10   9   8   7   6   5   4   3   2   1

This book is for all those who have struggled to make education within organizations effective and credible. It is our hope that this book will help you become the critical resource you need to be.

Contents

List of Tables, Figures, Templates, Exercises, and Survey

CD Contents

How to Use the Templates

Template 1.1. Corporate University Values

Template 2.1. Where Does Your Corporate University Jump In?

Template 2.2. Strategic Direction Guide

Template 3.1. Defining Scope

Template 4.1. Defining Your Governance Board

Template 4.2. Governance: Roles and Responsibilities

Template 5.1. Structure of Your Corporate University

Template 6.1. Hiring Plan

Template 7.1. Alternative Funding Models

Template 8.1. Curriculum Brainstorm Process

Template 9.1. Crafting Your Marketing Plan

Template 10.1. Stakeholders

Template 11.1. Strategic Vision

Corporate Education Survey

Acknowledgments

THIS BOOK is the result of years of collaboration, conversations, seminars, and discussions with countless people.

We are especially grateful to Sharadon Smith, who helped create an early version of this workbook, and for the inspiration of David Sibbet, president and founder of the Grove Consultants International, who taught us to think visually and how to use templates so effectively. We could not have done this book without the lessons we learned from Dr. Bob Miles, formerly of Georgia Tech, almost a decade ago. Bob was a pioneer in recognizing the value of corporate education as a tool for change. We have learned from books Mike Marquardt has written and from many conversations with him, and from always stimulating and often entertaining conversations with Jay Cross of the Internet Time Group.

We would also like to thank those who took time to listen, critique, discuss, and care about our work. These include Gary Bridges, Bill Daul, Sheldon Ellis, Dennis Morin, Libby Sartain, Dr. John Sullivan, and Eilif Trondsen.

And we are deeply grateful to Erik Foss, who spent hours and hours editing and formatting this work, checking the details, and adding insight. And to our families, who have patiently waited for us to finish.

Introduction

Getting the Most from This Resource

THE CORPORATE UNIVERSITY WORKBOOK will help you design, develop, and implement a corporate university in your organization quickly and effectively. It is the result of many years of work building corporate universities and working with clients to help them put corporate universities into action. Because of its straightforward, practical methodology, it should eliminate or reduce the need for expensive consultants. You will find this book useful whether you work in a small company or a large one, and whether you work in the nonprofit or for-profit sector.

Audience

This workbook is written for anyone who is faced with creating, developing, or improving the learning capacity of his or her organization. Whether you are a CEO or COO, a vice president of human resources, a training or development director or manager, or just someone who has been chartered with creating a better learning function for your organization, you will find this book useful. Regardless of your previous experience, you will be able to adapt the explanations, questionnaires, and templates to your organization.

How This Book Is Organized

Within the eleven chapters of this book, you will find a combination of best practices from the experiences of others and step-by-step processes that take you from the initial vision for your corporate university through to its implementation and assessment. Each chapter is designed to educate and inform you about a particular step in the design and implementation of the corporate university, and also to provide you with tools, templates, and activities that will help you, and those working with you, to think through the issues and create action plans. Most chapters offer brief case studies of successful and not so successful practices that existing corporate universities have gone through.

How to Use This Book

This is a hands-on book, put together so that you and a small team of associates can work through the creation and launch of your corporate university. We have tried to organize the chapters in the same order as that used by successful corporate universities. Therefore, we recommend that you start with Chapter One and take whatever time is needed to gather data or information, complete the activities, and flesh out the provided template. Then move on to Chapter Two and so forth. Each chapter is the springboard to the next one.

The Corporate Education Survey that is included in Chapter One is designed as a tool to help you calibrate the quality and characteristics of your current education efforts. Your score on this survey will provide some idea of how much effort will be required to move your education function to higher levels of usefulness and effectiveness. Take the survey yourself, give copies to all the people helping you design the corporate university, and distribute it to as many other people as you can. This composite view will give you two benefits: (1) it will establish a baseline view of your current activities (even if the view turns out to be painful to hear) and (2) it will give you an idea of which aspects of your education function need improvement. You can give this survey again after the corporate university has been in place for a while and track your progress.

What's on the CD-ROM?

The enclosed CD-ROM contains all the templates that are found in this book in a format suitable for printing, along with detailed explanations of how best to use the templates. Also included on the CD-ROM is the Corporate Education Survey for you to use in assessing organizational readiness.

A Website

We have also created a website to provide additional information and assistance as you design and build your corporate university. The website can be accessed at www.corpuworkbook.com.

Key Terms

To ensure that all readers have a common understanding of some key terms used in this workbook, we offer the following definitions of three frequently misunderstood terms:

Human Capital

There are three types of capital in organizations: financial, physical, and human. Financial and physical assets are well understood and are the basis of valuing organizations for the stock market. However, the employees and other stakeholders of any organization contribute their time, ideas, thoughts, and energy to the success of the organization. It is increasingly believed by experts, such as Peter Senge (1990) of MIT, who wrote *The Fifth Discipline,* and Thomas Davenport (1999), author of *Human Capital,* that this human contribution is the most significant to the success of any organization.

Learning Organization

A learning organization is an organization capable of profitably adapting to change, of engaging people in group problem solving, and of challenging the status quo to remain creative and competitive.

Stakeholders

Your stakeholders include everyone who learns from, contributes to, or has a financial stake in your organization's knowledge. Stakeholders include management, employees, customers, and suppliers.

Chapter 1

The Value of a Corporate University

A LOT OF TRAINING organizations have changed their name to "corporate university," but they really aren't doing things differently. A true corporate university (CU) has moved beyond training and education and into the daily challenge of getting results. It provides leadership in supporting people and processes to achieve bottom-line success for the organization.

Company A has received accolades as a "learning organization" for years. Its corporate university has committees, an annually reviewed curriculum, and a rotating plan for employees to take a set number of courses each year. Unfortunately, when you talk to the employees, they see "learning" as a time-consuming outtake from their daily work. The courses may have individual appeal but have little to do with their jobs. Their managers allow them to go, and give lip service to learning, but in reality they do not see the value. The days of this corporate university are numbered.

The value of QVC University is evident from the improved performance of QVC employees. The company's top executives conceived the university and implemented with a clear mission. As manager of human resources development, Susan Osciak defines the mission of QVC in terms of two goals: to provide employees with a venue to acquire business knowledge and to share best practices to foster continuous individual and organizational effectiveness.

Courses are defined by the question: *What do QVC people need to know about the business to increase their performance and role, jobs, and functions?* That question is asked and answered by a network of people in strategic positions across the organization. The value is clear from performance.

In this chapter, we will equip you with some background on how effective learning has added measurable value to all facets of organizations. You will learn how to build support for the corporate university, and how to prepare an effective business case for the creation of a corporate university. A survey at the end of this chapter will help you assess how your current educational activities are perceived, and will set the stage for preparing a solid business case for the corporate university.

What Is the Value of a Corporate University to Your Organization?

The corporate university is not primarily about how to deliver learning or how to carry forth the organization's culture. Rather it is about an emerging multidisciplinary view of learning as a key factor in organizational success. Most executives agree about the value of having a "learning organization," and statistics demonstrate that the best talent, innovation, and productivity are centered in organizations that grasp the meaning of learning at a deep level. Laurie Bassi and Daniel McMurrer, the chairwoman and chief research officer, respectively, at Knowledge Asset Management, a money management firm in Bethesda, Maryland, tracked for three years the performance of companies that spent at least twice as much as other firms on employee development. Their findings are clear: firms with the largest investments in people performed 17 to 35 percent better on the Standard & Poor's (S&P) index over that period. In addition, their research shows that companies that invest more money in training perform better on the stock market than companies that invest less (Bassi & McMurrer, 2002). Unfortunately, many organizations only understand learning on a surface level and make only cosmetic changes to old training and development departments.

A corporate university should:

- Have a direct and acknowledged impact on the business performance of the organization.

- Have a direct and acknowledged impact on individuals at the targeted level.

- Act as a hub for knowledge collection and dissemination.

- Integrate organization development, change management, training, career and leadership development, and knowledge management.

- Push individuals and the organization into thinking and acting outside of established or familiar patterns of learning—whether in what they learn or in how they learn it.

The corporate university is far more comprehensive than a training and development function and provides, in its ideal incarnation, a talent development process that supplies the organization the talent it needs to meet competitive challenges. Table 1.1 gives you some idea of how a corporate university differs from the traditional training and development function in its orientation and impact on profitability and perceived value.

TABLE 1.1

Corporate University Focus and Perceived Value

	Low ——— Contribution to Profit, Growth, or Efficiency ——— High	
Strategic (Focus or Orientation)	A CU with an academic and research emphasis. A focus on capturing and interpreting data and converting tacit to explicit knowledge.	A CU that integrates training, career development, knowledge management, organization development, change management with action learning, e-learning, and a focus on solving organizationwide issues or on attacking new areas.
Tactical	Traditional training and development. Focus on individual development and on content with only accidental or incidental impact on business goals and objectives.	Certification programs or formal curricula for leadership development, change management, or implementation of a business initiative.

The points above compose an ideal definition, and we do not know of any corporate university that has achieved all its elements. General Electric's John F. Welch Leadership Institute at Crotonville has probably come the closest. It has provided GE with the leadership it has needed to remain more than competitive in a time when its major competitors (Westinghouse, Raytheon, and others) have suffered. It pioneered "work out," a challenging leadership development process, and it has been the center of the development of future scenarios for strategic thinking.

Throughout this book, we will be working with you to help you define and position your corporate university. It will be essential for you to understand and continually prove that there is bottom-line value from the kind of learning you will offer through your corporate university.

Take a few minutes and complete Exercise 1.1 on page 8. This may seem like a trivial activity—after all, you simply may have been asked to create the corporate university with no obvious, compelling reason. However, by completing this activity you will force yourself, and we hope the others you include in writing this statement, to put into words the thoughts and ideas of all those who have had a hand in getting you to this point. You may need to interview a few of the executives in your organization or get a cross-section of interested employees to help you.

EXERCISE 1.1

The Value of Your Corporate University

Before continuing, please take a few moments to write what you believe will be the greatest value of a corporate university to your organization. In other words, why are you trying to create one at all?

_____

_____

_____

_____

_____

_____

_____

_____

_____

_____

_____

_____

_____

_____

_____

_____

_____

_____

_____

_____

_____

_____

_____

_____

The Value of Learning

As Shoshana Zuboff (1988) says in her book, *In the Age of the Smart Machine: The Future of Work and Power,* "Learning is the new form of labor" (p. 395). Indeed, more than 2.5 million manufacturing jobs have gone away since the start of the economic slowdown in the United States in the year 2000. Most of those jobs will not return. The western world is moving from manual-labor intensive, manufacturing-based economies to those based on the use of human intellect and thought.

Labor is now thought of as talent. Employees are moving from being regarded as a "pair-of-hands" that execute whatever a manager tells them to execute to being thought of as partners and contributors to the organization's success. In her book, *The Company of the Future,* Frances Cairncross (2002) of *The Economist* magazine says, "The value of the business increasingly lies not in factories or fleets of trucks, the sort of assets that appear on the balance sheet and are easy to value and manage. Instead, it lies in intangibles—brands, patents, franchises, software, research programs, ideas, and expertise" (p. 23). In other words, value lies in what individuals add using their skills, expertise, and creativity—not their muscles.

The most successful individuals and organizations are those who find ways to integrate learning into everyday activities. The workforce has to be continuously aware of changing circumstances and learn and adapt to changing needs.

The goal of the new corporate university leader must be to demonstrate and communicate the value of learning, and then build a system that can provide a forum for the learning—learning that positively influences business outcomes.

The role of learning in organizations has shifted from a peripheral activity, aimed mostly at giving workers manual skills or conceptual knowledge, to an activity aimed at more effectively making products or delivering services. More than ever before, those who can learn the fastest and adapt the easiest are the most successful. Small steel mills that learned how to recycle steel and iron competed with and won over large ones. Toyota's incredible ability to continuously learn from its mistakes and then modify its products has led it to world dominance in the automobile and small truck markets. The adjectives that describe the period we live in are words like *flexible, nimble, quick,* and *fluid.* Yet even though we recognize the importance of learning, most companies still have legacy training systems with structures, curricula, and processes that demonstrate none of these characteristics.

Return on Investment

Your ability to communicate and measure value—real or potential—is essential to constructing and sustaining a corporate university. You must build and present to your management and your stakeholders a solid business case that will carry your corporate university through difficult times.

For example, there is considerable evidence that the availability of formal training and even the opportunity for continuous learning are strong factors in employee retention, as shown below. Consider what the following information on corporate learning might mean for organizations striving to retain talented employees:

- In organizations today, career development is too often left to the individual. Hay Insight's employee opinion surveys suggest that only about one-half of employees feel that managers where they work display genuine interest in developing employees (Hay Group, 2002).

- The top four choices [of reasons for accepting first positions], in descending order of preference, were "opportunity for self-development," "challenge and responsibility," "freedom on the job," and "opportunity for advancement" (*Journal of Education for Business*, 2004, pp. 209-212).

- The percentage of people who say they will change jobs within a year is less for employees who receive job-related training (14 percent) than for those who do not (24 percent) (www.talentalliance.com).

Data like these can be used to help support your arguments for the corporate university. We all know that learning happens all the time in an informal and unstructured way, but no successful organization can rely on this informal learning happening in the right areas and at the right time to ensure its competitiveness. There is research in a broad array of areas that supports the need for a formal and integrated approach to organizational learning.

Support for Your Corporate University

Making a business case for your corporate university initiative will help you obtain and sustain management support, which is the pivotal factor in success. The corporate university can benefit the company's execution of its strategy by

- Identifying the needed competencies and skills for your workforce to implement organizational goals

- Translating those needs into specific development programs, which might include internal or external formal training, experiential learning, and coaching

- Harnessing the power of informal as well as formal learning opportunities, increasing as well as disseminating knowledge

- Helping capture and making explicit the tacit knowledge people have about how they do their jobs successfully

- Helping employees develop career directions and skills that are useful to the organization and that make them satisfied and productive

- Anticipating future skills, competencies, and abilities the organization will need to reach its aspirations and steering employees toward those areas

Deep Commitment

When a corporate university is new, especially if it is developed at the behest of an influential leader, it is easy to rally supporters and engage workers. However, sustaining support and engagement depends on a thoughtful and methodical process of building relationships and demonstrating value. The following are some tips about how to communicate the value of your corporate university from the onset:

- Know how you are perceived. Use the survey at the end of this chapter and gain an understanding of how others—ordinary employees and management—see what you are currently doing. Their answers will give you insight into where you should focus your communication and will help you in deciding on your strategic direction.

- Do not take anyone by surprise. Before your formal presentation about why a corporate university makes sense, be sure that you have talked to all key players to hear their views. Probe them for their concerns and their hopes. When appropriate, refer to a specific person's contribution of an idea or his or her concern over an issue in your presentation(s).

- Talk the business. Demonstrate that you are knowledgeable about the business, and avoid using HR or training lingo. Speak about results, not about activities.

- Talk about benefits, not features. For example, don't talk about classes or delivery methods (at least not initially); talk about skill gaps and how they can be closed to improve the productivity of employees or how the organization will profit by having better-skilled employees.

- Ask for the listener's commitment confidently. Expect an answer and get him or her to commit to a timeline for moving forward.

- You've heard the old adage, "underpromise and overdeliver." It holds true. Find some areas where you can make a visible impact and deliver. Pick low-hanging fruit and then make it happen.

- It often is more effective to work with managers who are excited and want your help. Spending too much time on those who are negative or naysayers can sap your energy. They can be won over later as they see the results you are achieving.

- Develop a name for your corporate university that will resonate with your company's culture. Frequently tie your efforts to the name selected so that you develop a "brand image."

- By getting out into the business and carefully listening to employees from all levels and functions, you can get specific ideas about what the university can accomplish that will be useful to these stakeholders. When you include these ideas in your presentation you will enjoy greater support and limit resistance.

First Steps Toward Creating Your Corporate University

The following are three critical steps to take on your way toward building your successful corporate university.

Step 1. Develop a Business Case for Your Corporate University

Arrange a meeting with the major supporters of the corporate university. Fill out Template 1.1 with bullets outlining your business case for the corporate university. Use this as a visual communication tool to clarify your reasons for moving forward.

Also, talk to people in your organization who are critical to your corporate university's success (whether they are named or not); find out their definition of and their expectations for a corporate university. Write the consensus view and what you think is right or wrong about your company's current approach or view of training and employee development.

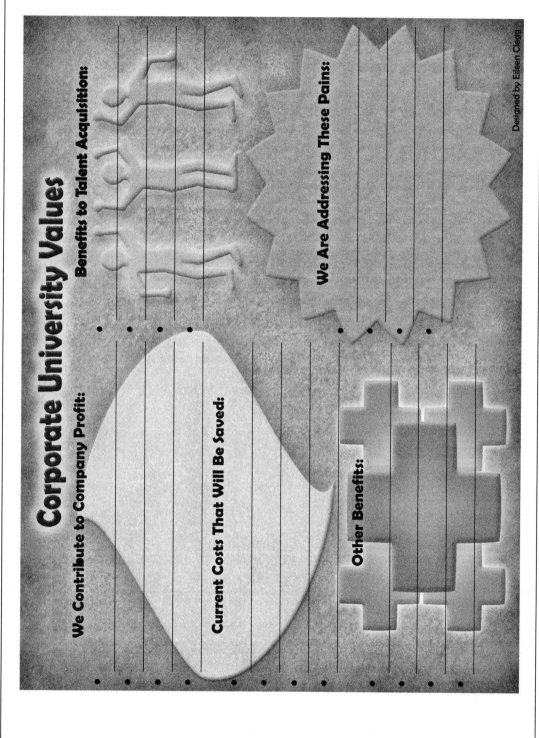

Corporate University Values

We Contribute to Company Profit:

Benefits to Talent Acquisition:

Current Costs That Will Be Saved:

We Are Addressing These Pains:

Other Benefits:

Designed by Eileen Clegg

Key Items to Have in a Compelling Business Presentation

This is an outline of the elements that will have the most positive impact on your audience as you begin to make a presentation about your corporate university.

- Provide a brief background of your organization's training history and what has happened to lead you to the idea of a corporate university. This will establish context and history.

- Point out the problem or issue you will address with the corporate university. Make a case that there is a problem by using facts, figures, and examples.

- Outline the benefit(s) of eliminating the problem or issue. What would happen if this issue did not exist? Paint a vision of what could be. Why is the corporate university the best way to solve this problem or address this issue?

- Lay out your solution. Make this as simple yet as credible as possible. Keep it short and include how you will measure your success.

- Anticipate and be able to answer questions like these:

  - Why can *you* solve this better than some other person or group?

  - How will we know if you are successful?

  - We tried something like this in the past, and it didn't work. Why should we try again?

  - Isn't this just too far-fetched, too expensive, too faddish?

- Ask for the investment and the go-ahead in terms of these benefits. For example, although it will cost you to do this, your net return, after paying back this investment, will be higher.

Prepare a Written Document

After you have the information you need to address the points raised above, you should create a formal written business case. This might be a few Power-Point slides or a white paper that outlines what benefits and value creating a corporate university will bring to your organization. Ideally, you will present this business case to the people who are chartering you, and you will be able to determine whether your arguments are strong enough and if your data are compelling enough for you to get their support.

Step 2. Complete the Corporate Education Survey—Then Take It Again

Complete the Corporate Education Survey on pages 15–17. The corporate education survey is designed to be used as a tool to provide an initial

Corporate Education Survey

Introduction

It is important to know how your training and development function is perceived by management and the employees in your organization. Effectiveness and success are closely tied to perception. Without an objective view of how you are perceived, it will be difficult to make changes that are meaningful and that will result in your function's gaining credibility and effectiveness.

This survey is designed to help you calibrate the quality and characteristics of your current education efforts. Your score on this survey will provide some idea of how much effort will be required to move your education function to higher levels of usefulness and effectiveness.

Take the survey yourself, give copies to all the people helping you design the corporate university, and distribute it to as many other people as you can. The more people you can get to take the survey, the more reliable your results will be. A broad, composite view will give you two benefits: (1) it will establish a baseline view of your current activities (even if the view turns out to be painful to hear) and (2) it will give you an idea of which aspects of your education function need improvement and where to focus your improvement activities.

You can repeat this survey after the corporate university has been in place for a while and track your progress. In fact, this survey could be given periodically to continue to track your progress.

Instructions

For each of the following, please rate your level of agreement using a 1–4 scale, where 1 = strongly disagree and 4 = strongly agree. Enter 0 if you don't know or the question is not applicable. Place your rating number in the space provided for each question. When you have finished, add up all the scores and review your result in the Scorecard below.

Strongly disagree	Somewhat disagree	Somewhat agree	Strongly agree	Don't know/ Not applicable
1	2	3	4	0

_____ 1. Our training and development staff have a clearly defined strategy regarding our objectives, and how and when they will be achieved.

_____ 2. Our training and development function goals are related directly to key business goals of our organization.

_____ 3. All employees clearly understand who receives the benefits of the training and development function and why.

_____ 4. The training and development function's primary stakeholders are clearly defined.

_____ 5. Our training and development function's organizational structure enables us to efficiently develop and deliver our services to meet our business objectives.

_____ 6. Our training and development function has a governing structure that makes major decisions.

_____ 7. The budgeting process is well understood and clear to all the stakeholders of the training and development function.

_____ 8. The people who staff the training and development function have strong business knowledge.

Corporate Education Survey, Cont'd

_____ 9. Our training and development function has a communication process we use to publicize to all employees how we contribute to profitability or have improved employee productivity.

_____ 10. The curriculum is thoughtfully developed to achieve specific, measurable business goals.

_____ 11. The training and development function has developed a set of measures or metrics used to gauge the performance of the department.

_____ 12. We regularly report our performance metrics to senior management.

_____ 13. Curricula are often delivered by a combination of methods including e-learning, on-the-job training, action learning, and other methods.

_____ 14. We report how training and development has helped the company achieve its business goals.

_____ 15. Our training and development staff is credible to the line management and employees.

_____ 16. There are explicit financial metrics and processes for both tracking and reporting financial performance.

_____ 17. Our processes and structure for funding the training and development function within our organization are clearly defined and understood.

_____ 18. There is a governing person or board to guide the training and development function and provide advice and support.

_____ 19. Our training and development organizational structure is practical, effective, and easy to operate in.

_____ 20. Our governance board provides training and development management the flexibility to adapt to changing circumstances.

_____ 21. Our training and development function's charter is clear to the rest of the company—everyone can express why there is a corporate university and what it does.

_____ 22. Our training and development function has a robust and updated intranet (or internally accessed website) that communicates its activities, plans, and all information employees need in order to effectively utilize the department.

_____ 23. Our training and development function stakeholders are in agreement regarding the range of services offered.

_____ 24. Line managers understand where to go or where to send their employees for educational and learning services.

_____ 25. Line managers in our organization understand how the training and development function can help them achieve their business goals.

_____ 26. The way decisions are made about learning priorities is clear to all stakeholders.

_____ 27. Our training and development function is ultimately responsible to a single person or committee, which also has financial control.

_____ 28. There is a budgeting cycle, and special projects can be funded outside this cycle when necessary.

Corporate Education Survey, Cont'd

_____ 29. Our training and development function staff spend at least half of the time directly involved with the business, on customer needs, or on product or service issues.

_____ 30. Portions of the curricula are delivered by line managers, content experts, and other employees who are not part of our training and development function.

_____ 31. We have a set of metrics or a scorecard that demonstrates how all stakeholders benefit from the training and development function.

_____ 32. Our training and development function is not asked to deliver training outside the area(s) for which we are financed and staffed.

_____ 33. Our metrics measure both efficiency (that is, speed, cost) and effectiveness (that is, goals achieved, strategies implemented) of our training and development function.

_____ 34. Our training and development function has a repository or database containing key learnings, vital strategic data, competitive data, and other material that can assist decision making and improve learning.

_____ 35. We have a process for receiving feedback regarding training staff effectiveness and credibility.

_____ 36. Our curriculum is designed to encourage internal development function in order to reduce the need for external hiring.

Scoring

Add all numbers and enter the total here: _____

Scorecard

133–144: Congratulations. Only a handful of learning organizations have achieved this level of strategic integration and effectiveness. Be sure you continue to keep up with a rapidly changing world!

120–132: With some attention to the areas where you scored a "3" or lower, you can rise to the top level. You are to be congratulated on a great job of steering your learning organization to this level.

90–119: You are clearly on the road to effectiveness. With the help of this book and a little work on the areas where you scored a "1" or "2," you can easily move up this scale. If you gave any question a "0," make sure you find out whatever it is you don't know or read the chapters in this book that will guide you in putting in place a better practice.

77–89: You've got a ways to go, but the good news is that you now have an idea where you should focus your efforts. Start with the areas where your scores were "1" or "2," as these will bring you the fastest improvements. If you gave any question a "0," take the time to learn enough to be able to rate the item. This book will guide you through some of the tough spots.

76 or below: Most likely you are just getting started or are growing a small organization. You probably marked several items with "0's." This book will be an invaluable guide as you move through the development function and growth of your learning organization.

understanding about how you are currently being perceived. We recommend you take the survey and distribute it as widely as possible (a reproducible copy is included on the accompanying CD) within your organization to get a baseline understanding of how your current function is perceived among stakeholders and the management team.

Although the answers will provide you insight during the design phase of your corporate university, the survey should be used again after the corporate university has been operating for a while. We recommend that after one year you distribute the survey again and compare the results to the first version of the survey.

Step 3. Build Your Design Team

Architecting and building a corporate university is a collective activity that should involve a wide range of people. Throughout this book, we will refer to a steering committee or design team, which you should assemble as you embark on this journey. A design team typically consists of seven to ten people chosen for their vision, understanding of the organization, support for learning and employee development, and their influence in the organization.

Effective design teams often include several senior HR people, one or two line managers, a financial person, and several people from the training and development staff, if one exists. It is possible to include outside experts or consultants, but this is not necessary. Small organizations should use a variety of line managers and senior-level employees and may want to include consultants from outside.

The charter of this team is to help you work through this book and lay out the business case and other elements necessary for a successful launch. Team members need to have skills, influence, and the time to investigate areas where you need information or data. This needs to be a senior-level team with strategic focus. The subsequent chapters will define the specific tasks for which your team should provide assistance.

After the initial design phase, this team may be disbanded or it may break off into a subteam with a more focused charter. Some members may end up as part of the governance structure of the corporate university, although this is not usually the case.

Conclusion

Understanding and articulating the value of your corporate university will provide the foundation you need to move forward. Creating a written business case outlining expected benefits of the corporate university should have deepened your thinking and engaged others. You now have a detailed, compelling, and fact-based explanation for why you are embarking on this task, and you should be able to engage others in the steps ahead. Your next task is establishing your strategy and direction.

Chapter 2

Planning the Corporate University
Strategy and Direction

> All grand strategies eventually deteriorate into work.
>
> —PETER DRUCKER

Company B always had a reputation for a great culture, was very profitable and successful, had grown rapidly over a ten-year period, and then decided to put in place a corporate university. However, it lacked a clear mission or charter. The initial concept was to use the term *corporate university* as a recruiting tool to attract people to the corporation and as a way to organize some disparate departmental training functions under a common name. The result was the renaming of a training department, the addition of some courses offered corporatewide, and some reduction in staff due to consolidation. However, other than cost savings and the name change, very little was fundamentally different. It did not have any overarching goal and it was not connected to business results in any visible way. As a result, within two years of being established, it had little to no support from management, little interest from employees, and has since been reduced to a small number of people with very little impact on the organization.

Defense Acquisition University (DAU) is the Department of Defense's CUBIC-Award winning university, headed by Frank Anderson. The Corporate University Best in Class (CUBIC) Awards were established by the International Quality and Productivity Center (IQPC) to honor, recognize, and promote corporate universities that represent true best practices. Mr. Anderson's charter in creating the corporate university was driven by the need for change. DAU was chartered to deal with the acquisition needs of a twenty-first century army and to educate leadership on how to best use the changing methodologies of acquisition. Historically the military has moved slowly and bureaucratically and tended to have long planning cycles, but the twenty-first century conflicts in Afghanistan and Iraq have underlined the need to be prepared quickly—to "interact with surprises." Therefore, the challenge to DAU was to change and educate. How do you help a huge, sclerotic organization change overnight? That was the core challenge. Although there is no way to prove causality, DAU's ability to provide education and distribute knowledge about new acquisition methods helped the Army meet the rapid supply requirements of Afghanistan and Iraq. DAU's grand mission—to streamline and change the way the military acquires products—has had strong support from senior defense administration leadership. It continues to receive a healthy budget, and remains an integral part of U.S. Department of Defense strategy.

FOCUS AND DIRECTION are keys to almost everything we do, and in architecting a corporate university they are critical. Without focus and direction, you are a rudderless ship, sailing around and around without going anywhere. The corporate university has to have a well-defined purpose and a set of specific goals to achieve. Without those, its success, and yours, will be uncertain. This chapter is about choosing your strategic direction from a variety of possibilities.

The Importance of Strategy

I open my seminars for corporate university leaders by asking everyone to go dig a hole for me. They look at me strangely, asking, "Why? Aren't we here to learn about corporate universities?" Then the questions begin to fly. They ask me where to dig and with what tools and how big, and so on. I do this exercise to make it clear to them how strategy is core to their success when organizational leadership says, "Start a corporate university," or even when they themselves come up with the concept. Before anything else, you need to understand why you are going to create one, what it will accomplish, and for whom, how, and when.

If your senior management has said to you, "Create a corporate university," you need to spend an appropriate amount of time with whoever told you that, and with other stakeholders, to identify the motivations and long-term reasons for wanting to create this corporate university.

In order to have sustainability, you must have a long-term core mission that makes sense to leadership and employees. We often forget that when employees know they are learning concepts and skills that can be put into use, they influence leadership to provide more resources and support. Clear strategic direction that can be explained to anyone in a few sentences enhances your chances of success.

To help you choose your strategic direction, complete Exercise 2.1 on page 22.

Strategy Is Fundamental: Form Follows Function

No organization, function, or department can successfully implement change or achieve its goals unless its long-term purpose is clearly defined. Ideally, a corporate university is launched with a specific mission aligned to help the organization achieve its business objectives. For example, the U.S. Defense Department faced unprecedented challenges brought by world events that led to decisions by administration and Congress requiring a more nimble military. Consequently, the mission of Defense Acquisition

EXERCISE 2.1

Selecting a Strategic Direction

In our experience, there are only four—maybe five—major strategic approaches that corporate universities fulfill. This exercise will help you identify the one or two that are most likely to be useful to your organization. Have members of the design team fill out this form on their own, knowing they will discuss their choices with the other team members and again with your stakeholders and your organization's key leadership.

Once everyone has completed this, engage in an active discussion about why they chose the ones they did. The goal should be for the design team to understand very deeply the organization's needs and come to consensus. Your final agreed-on choices should be presented to senior management for their review and approval.

This may seem like a trivial activity, but the first few activities that you will be doing in this book are actually building the foundation of understanding and agreement that everything else, including your eventual success or failure, will depend on.

The most pressing need we have as an organization is to (choose only ONE):

1. Find or develop skilled employees.

2. Develop a top-notch management team.

3. Help our customers understand our products and services.

4. Effect wide-scale change in the way we think and do business.

5. Find ways to grow our company.

6. Experiment with new approaches to learning.

7. Improve customer service and satisfaction.

8. Enter new markets or new geographies.

9. Move away from traditional ways of thinking.

10. Work with the academic world to explore and use new technologies.

The next most important need is to (choose only ONE):

1. Find or develop skilled employees.

2. Develop a top-notch management team.

3. Help our customers understand our products and services.

4. Effect wide-scale change in the way we think and do business.

5. Find ways to grow our company.

6. Experiment with new approaches to learning.

7. Improve customer service and satisfaction.

8. Enter new markets or new geographies.

9. Move away from traditional ways of thinking.

10. Work with the academic world to explore and use new technologies.

EXERCISE 2.1, Cont'd

Selecting a Strategic Direction

If you chose:

Statements 1 or 2: Skill and Development Focus. These signal that development of employee skills and competencies is a key need. The focus of the university can be on developing skill-building programs and on finding opportunities to give employees training and experience in new areas. Activities might include course work but also action learning projects and experiential development. It is important to make sure this is the KEY need your organization has. It is a common mistake to think that skills are the problem when it is really the fear of change or the need for innovative thinking.

Statements 3 or 7: External Customer Focus. These show that you need to concentrate on the customers you already have. Customers may need a better understanding of your products or services, or they may want to learn how you are dealing with quality and service issues. You may want to develop special programs for them or include them in programs you already have for employees. However, you may also simply want to spend time with customers in strategic conversations or at events and activities sponsored by the university.

Statements 4 or 8: Change Management Focus. These reflect the need for change and for moving on to new areas. This is when large-scale change programs are appropriate and can get the whole company aligned in a new direction. These types of corporate university orientations require top management support and involvement. If you do not have that, don't try this approach. Usually programs that promote change are fast-paced and high-level. There are simulations, visioning courses, work techniques, and other methods that have been successfully used to drive change.

Statements 5 or 9: Strategic/Business Focus. These indicate a need to grow and move into territory that your organization has never been in. In this situation, special seminars and courses on growth, the new market space, and innovation and creativity are appropriate. This strategic orientation is often coupled with the change orientation.

Statements 6 or 10: Academic Research Focus. These indicate a think-tank approach and one that is more focused on exploring new territory in a theoretical way than in finding immediate practical applications. Be sure that this is the real intent of senior management. Most successful corporate universities use this as a minor or secondary strategy, giving priority to one of the other approaches.

University (DAU) was clear: help the army acquire supplies and material more quickly. The strategic direction DAU chose was, at least initially, change management. That choice became the foundation upon which all strategic decisions were made within the corporate university. However, I have been in many companies where the corporate university was not clearly chartered and where its energy was dissipated in many directions.

Following Exercise 2.1, you should have a good idea of what your strategic focus is or could be. If you have given equal importance to everything, you need to spend more time clarifying your charter and your mission. However, specific items should have clearly taken precedence. If you have been working with senior leadership, or have put your thinking through a group process, then you have also increased the chances that you have chosen the best approach for your organization.

As corporate universities have evolved over the past several years, a number of primary strategic orientations have been identified. I have tried to categorize and comment on them in Table 2.1. One of these strategic directions is probably "right" for your organization.

TABLE 2.1

Corporate Education Focus Areas

Strategic Driver	Definition	Characteristics
Skill & Development Focus (Qualification)		
Skill	Focus on developing and maintaining skills of employees. Drives excellence across a discipline, e.g., financial or engineering expertise and skill updating.	May be localized in a division. Not necessarily directly tied to corporate strategy.
External Customer Focus (Relationship)		
Customer	Focus on delivering technical skills to customers, vendors, suppliers, or partners. Focus on delivering education as a way to increase customer loyalty, use of service/product, or as a way to establish a relationship.	May generate a positive cash flow or may be a service to customers where cost is built into product/service pricing.
Change Management Focus		
Change agent	Primary charter is to create/drive organizationwide change or transformation.	Focus on organizational performance. Team and group collaboration. Mediation, dialogue, and learning of organization skills.
Strategic Business Focus (Accomplishment)		
Business need	Pushes strategy and corporate initiatives.	Owned by CEO/senior management. Part of or reports to corporate headquarters.
Research (Academic)		
Future	Focus on future needs and on finding underlying causes/drivers/competences for success.	Emerging area for a few corporate universities. Might be a secondary function included in a CU with one of the approaches above.

Skill and Development Focused

This approach also has two major subcategories. The first is leadership development, which many organizations have made the core of their corporate university strategy. The second is a broader approach that places emphasis on building and maintaining the skills of employees in general. Both use e-learning and other emerging delivery methods to improve availability and access.

Leadership Development Driven

The prototype for this strategic focus is General Electric's Management Development Institute at Crotonville, New York. This institute has focused on developing managers and leaders for General Electric for decades. It has been almost exclusively the tool of the CEO, Jack Welch, for orienting and assimilating new managers to the company. It has also been the tool for driving change and initiatives using programs such as Workout and Change Acceleration Process. Workout got hundreds of GE leaders involved in brainstorming and discussing ways to improve the productivity and effectiveness of their work. Change Acceleration Process is a similar but more structured effort to enlist the power of hundreds of employees to make change take place and make change last. Both programs are products of Crotonville. Corporate universities with CEO-level support and a single primary focus on leadership development are usually very successful and produce great internal management strength.

Broad-Based Competency Development

This category is what almost every university does at some level, but for some this is all they do. One example is McDonald's University. It is focused on teaching the managers of McDonald's restaurants how to prepare food and run their restaurant. It also offers education and skill building to a wide variety of other employees. The university maintains a mock restaurant and uses modern equipment to teach skills and customer service.

Challenges

Everyone understands the need for employees to have up-to-date skills, so the development approach is a popular beginning approach for a corporate university. This is usually perceived as an easier choice to implement because it is probably what you have already been doing. Yet in most cases, it has the least impact on the organization. It doesn't make a statement to the employees that anything is different about the corporate university, and it is usually aimed at helping employees maintain current practices and methods. One of the ways a corporate university can show value is by identifying the competencies that will be needed in the near future because of manufacturing, technical, business, or geographical changes and developing competency training for those. For example, Motorola University developed Six Sigma training for its internal employees well before anyone outside of Motorola had even heard the term and before the training was available to outside customers. General Electric, likewise, developed new approaches to leadership development through its Workout program and pioneered teaching those skills to gain competitive advantage.

However, it will still be necessary to ensure that the more ordinary skills and competencies of employees are not neglected. While you are developing the corporate university, you might look at finding other ways to deliver your usual training programs. Some companies ask the operating units to take over the responsibility for skills training. At National Semiconductor, the response was to find an outsource partner to take on the job of individual employee development, combined with a shift of responsibility for this to the divisions and business units rather than the corporate function. This freed up time and resources for a focus on a more strategic need—change management.

External Customer Focused

Some corporate universities are investing in customer education on different levels and in different areas. These include education in product understanding and use, technical education (certification as Microsoft or Cisco Systems offer), and assistance to customers to achieve success so that they will be bigger purchasers of products or services.

Motorola and General Electric have done the latter for many years. Motorola has offered its customers quality training and certification, and General Electric has offered its expertise in change management. Cisco Systems, Sun Microsystems, and Microsoft have extensive customer education and certification programs for their products. These programs are revenue generators and increase the use of their products.

One of the byproducts of customer education is that the educational materials are available for internal employees, as well. This means that with little additional effort many educational products can serve two audiences and keep costs low.

Change Management Focused

Another form of corporate university concentrates its efforts on driving change or on facilitating a complete transformation process for a company.

This is often a transitory role as a company embarks on a new strategy or is in the process of merger or acquisition. The university may then go through a metamorphosis from this type to being an initiative-driven or skill-provider type.

National Semiconductor used National Semiconductor University to drive a Leading Change program through the company that helped lead to a financial turnaround in the mid-1990s. Today, the university is more focused on leadership and skill development but retains its ability to respond whenever needed to bring about change.

The focus on helping managers and employees understand and deal with vast change, internally or in the marketplace or both, is a second definition of a corporate university. The change-management focused corporate university has to help people understand and interpret the emerging new environment, help the entire organization move through the phases of change, provide new capabilities and skills to meet the new challenges, and be extremely well aligned with future thinking.

Strategic Business Focus

Strategic business focus can be divided into two subfocus areas: those that are driven by some particular business need and take on the form of an initiative or project, and those that are driven by the need to develop some new or emerging segment of business.

Initiative Driven

This type of university is usually recognized because its primary public activity is driving a corporatewide initiative or business plan or project. This is often an initiative that the CEO is passionate about and which is being cascaded throughout the company. It is an appropriate and excellent model when there are "great things afoot."

Originally, Motorola University used this approach to very successfully drive the quality initiative throughout Motorola. At the same time, Motorola U was also involved in strategic planning and in helping the company cope with expansion into China and other parts of the world. It pioneered the idea of bringing focus to one or two issues and putting a structure in place to facilitate delivering the content, coaching the implementation, and building understanding and acceptance of the issues with management and the employees. Motorola U did not do individual skill training, competency development, or leadership development outside of the context of the quality initiative.

Examples of business initiatives include such things as globalization, productivity, process improvement, and empowerment. This turns out to be one of the most important of the emerging definitions of a corporate university.

Business Development Driven

A few universities are chartered to help develop business opportunities or to guide an exploration process to determine what is possible. When an organization decides to embark on a particular business strategy—for example, opening several international offices—the corporate university can prepare employees for their role, help educate employees about the new country, do research on competition and on recruiting and development, and generally support the process in a value-added way. Some companies make this the function of the marketing department, but by putting it into a corporate university (or by partnering), leadership development, collaboration skills, teamwork, and other skills get embedded into the project team and the result is far more synergistic than if the project were implemented as a marketing or R&D effort alone.

One example of this type of strategy is QVC University, whose mission is "to provide employees with a venue to acquire business knowledge and share best practices to foster continuous individual and organization effectiveness." Of course, this approach requires a staff with deep business, marketing, and strategic skills. If your corporate university is to be business development driven, you will need to be connected to the corporate product or service strategies, understand how employee skills contribute to the success of that strategy, and know what future strategies are being planned so that you can have people prepared and ready to take on the new challenges.

Research or Academic Focused

A very few corporate universities are exploring areas that are usually reserved for research labs in universities or involve topics that are considered too theoretical for the corporate environment. Examples of these activities include the work of Wayne Hodgins, a strategic futurist and director of Worldwide Learning Strategies at AutoDesk, Inc. Wayne runs a website called Learnativity, dedicated to exploring ways people can learn faster and more thoroughly the things they need to make organizations effective. Another example is the Bank of Montreal's Institute for Learning, which has researched creativity, whether or not it is possible to develop creative skills, and how to do that.

When Do You Use These Approaches?

The role of the corporate university is continually in flux. You will use different approaches at different times. Almost all corporate universities that have existed for more than five years have gone through metamorphoses from time to time. Many start out as skill and competency focused and then morph into organizations driving change, building a new leadership team, or assisting in the entry to a new market. The governance committee and the corporate university's leadership have to be alert, aware of organizational shifts, and prepared to change direction as needed.

When is a change management strategy appropriate? When you, the CEO, or senior management begin to perceive that things in your business space are under stress or changing, that competitors are gaining market share, or that profits are down. The corporate university can help management see these trends, often by acting as the catalyst for discussions and even creative debates about organizational decisions or competitor market moves. For example, a medium-sized manufacturer of implantable medical devices used its internal learning function to help the senior team engage in discussion and debate over several alternate possible product strategies. The learning function put together discussion articles and organized research and speakers so that various aspects of each decision was better understood than it had been using the usual process, where a few key executives made the decisions. By acting as the neutral focal point for conversation, several new approaches were agreed on that led to significant market success. As an alternative, the corporate university can simply be the instrument to implement a change process once others in the organization see the need for a new direction.

When do you pursue a business development approach? When you find your management focused on introducing a new product or a new technology or are about to make an acquisition. This approach is also vital when you are moving into a new geographical space. New product introduction, new geographies, and mergers and acquisitions are triggers that signal the need for new understanding, skills, and competencies—ones that the organization most likely does not have. If the corporate university is part of the thinking that has led to these new directions, it can help current employees adapt and lower the need for outside hiring. It also increases employee confidence in the organization, lowers turnover, and improves morale.

When do you just focus on competency development? Once new skills have been identified and you are well on the way toward putting them universally in place, then your charter moves to one of more rapidly accelerating the development of skills, ensuring all employees have and maintain those skills.

When do you focus on external customers? Occasionally, organizations choose to look outside, taking their vision and competencies to a larger group of stakeholders, such as suppliers and customers. Sometimes this is in response to customer requests for support and training, and sometimes it is seen as a way to increase revenue. It is often done "on the side" while internal development is also under way.

When is the research or academic model appropriate? Whenever an organization faces uncertainty or when strategic situations require approaches that are not generally understood or even known, it is helpful to have the capability to explore this new territory in a constructive and experimental way. By engaging the corporate university to involve executives and other employees in scenario planning, simulations, or other future-oriented activities, new ideas emerge. These can give a competitive advantage to an organization. For example, Dow Chemical has been exploring how to put teams together that work more efficiently. By uncovering the patterns of behavior of individuals in successful and not so successful teams, patterns around individual competencies and skills are uncovered. Although this is early research, the results promise to improve Dow's productivity and ability to beat the competition.

Getting the Picture

Chances are you received a mandate to create a corporate university from someone who believes it's a good idea but who does not have a detailed picture. In most cases, it will be up to you to not just give answers but also to come up with the questions that have not been posed.

Strategic Requirements

Template 2.1 can be completed individually or with a group of stakeholders. We recommend that you do this with your design team after each team member has completed his or her own template. By sharing the various approaches, you will end up with a richer and more thorough end product and will stimulate thinking and discussion.

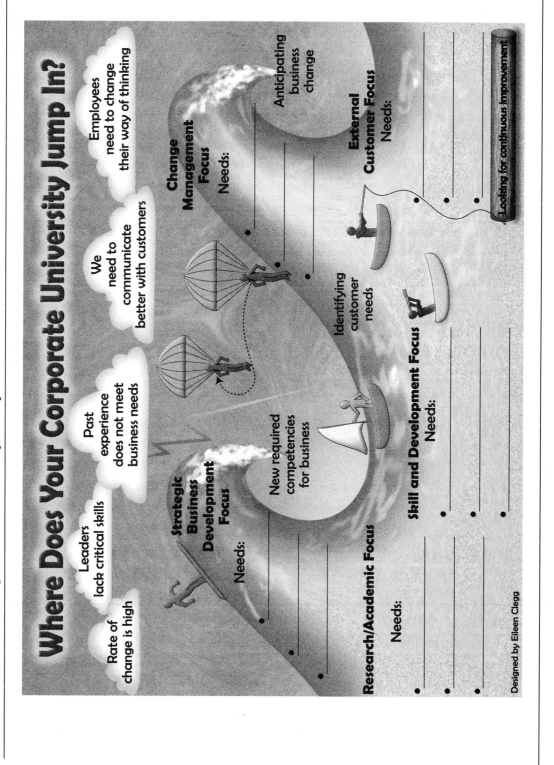

Where Does Your Corporate University Jump In?

Rate of change is high

Leaders lack critical skills

Past experience does not meet business needs

We need to communicate better with customers

Employees need to change their way of thinking

Strategic Business Development Focus

Needs:

New required competencies for business

Change Management Focus

Needs:

Anticipating business change

Identifying customer needs

Research/Academic Focus

Needs:

Skill and Development Focus

Needs:

External Customer Focus

Needs:

Looking for continuous improvement

Designed by Eileen Clegg

Strategic Direction

After considering the takeaways from the meeting on strategic requirements and reviewing this chapter in light of that input, you will be ready to take your strategic requirements to the next level. At this point it should be possible to create a vision map with the overall "big picture" of your corporate university—a picture that will guide your decisions ahead. Again, bring together your design team and add any other key stakeholders to develop the vision map. Use Template 2.2 as a wall chart visual to guide and capture your discussion.

Review the Strategic Requirements template (Template 2.1) in a meeting with your planning team to decide which strategy you will adopt. Although you have already thought through the different strategic directions, based on your company's current needs, it is best to start with a blank template in your team meeting to determine what others see as the best direction. Be open-minded but also use this opportunity to make your position clear, even as you are fine-tuning it with the input of others.

Conclusion

At this point you should have a general picture of where you are going—and why—with your corporate university. Remember that your strategy and direction are likely to change at some point in the future, but for now, they will provide the basis for many decisions. Your vision itself should be broad and strong enough to remain constant, even as your corporate university changes and grows, although the road map and details will constantly change. With the "big picture" established, you will be ready to move into the mechanics—scope and operating principles—in the next chapter.

Strategic Direction Guide

Strategic Direction Guide

Our Vision:

Specific Steps/Goals:

Strengths:

Corporate Culture:

Barriers:

Our Roots:

Abilities:

Designed by Eileen Clegg

Chapter 3

Determining the Scope, Stakeholders, and Operating Principles

YOUR OPERATING PRINCIPLES are those basic assumptions about education, training, and learning that all your decisions are made around, consciously or unconsciously. Your scope is the reach of your corporate university—the levels of employees who will benefit. Your stakeholders include everyone who learns from, contributes to, or has a financial stake in your organization's knowledge.

Corporate university director Paula worked for a multinational company with a large corporate university. It operated with a clear charter focused on change management at the leadership level. It was well resourced, had been in existence for several years, and was respected by all employees. Paula left that organization for an opportunity to set up a corporate university in a smaller firm. She thought the freedom and size would be advantageous and allow her to explore areas she couldn't in the larger organization. Without creating a governance committee and without a deep understanding of the corporate culture, she developed a corporate university chartered to offer something for everyone. She assumed that funding and other resources would be forthcoming. However, it was a tough sell in this small and practical organization. She had tried to get top management to give her their thoughts, but it was difficult to get any time with the top executives and they really had not addressed the question of scope or resources themselves. They did not realize that her approach was at odds with theirs until she already had a complete plan. When she unveiled her plan for the corporate university to serve the full workforce, they did not agree with her approach and felt she did not understand the organization. Soon after that, she was asked to resign. They then used external consultants to begin a much smaller, highly focused corporate university chartered with leadership development. The corporate university that emerged is small, centralized, and coordinated from within but primarily reliant on external faculty.

QVC University started with two top leaders sitting down at lunch and envisioning what kind of corporate university would best support the company's development. From the beginning, the corporate university focused on alignment with business goals. The scope was clear, the principles were clear, and the target group was identified. With content tied to the business's bottom line, top leadership became engaged with the corporate university. The initial vision was to create value-added courses to support the business and harness the knowledge of QVC, invest in intellectual assets in merchandising and strategy, and plow the knowledge of managers and executives back into the business. Having a clear idea of their scope enabled them to move fast and build relationships that would make their corporate university a success. The vision is growing, with organizational leadership identifying future business direction that affects the content and delivery of courses. Enabling this growth is continuous engagement with people throughout the company.

One of the first issues that you will have to decide is how open your corporate university will be. Will it offer development to everyone in your organization or will it have a narrower focus? Simultaneously, you will have to determine who will benefit from the corporate university—who has an investment in its success—and what the core principles and values will be that drive you forward. This chapter addresses these issues and, by using a series of templates and exercises, helps you figure them out.

Determining Your Scope, Stakeholders, and Operating Principles

For the purposes of this chapter, the *stakeholders* of the corporate university are the people who receive its benefits. *Scope* has to do with geographic and organizational breadth. Which company locations will be served? Which job categories and functions? *Operating principles* are the actual assumptions you make about who is served and how.

Every organization makes assumptions—usually implicit in their actions, but not articulated well—about people and their development. For example, organizations such as IBM operated for more than half a century with the primary philosophy that hiring new college graduates and developing them internally was the best way to build IBM's capabilities. Other organizations have chosen to hire experienced people and have not devoted any significant resources to development. You can use Exercise 3.1 on page 36 to help you think about your organization's basic philosophy about people and development.

EXERCISE 3.1

Stakeholders and Scope

Put a check mark in front of each statement below that completely fits with your view of how the organization feels about the statement or how management would view that statement.

_____ Everyone in the company should receive benefits from the corporate university.

_____ Only managers should receive benefits from the corporate university.

_____ Managers do not need development from a corporate university—experience and a few external classes are enough.

_____ We should hire people right out of college and be responsible for their training and career development.

_____ Experienced hires do not need significant development—our training function does a good enough job.

_____ Everyone needs training, but managers really need the higher-level corporate university kind of education and development.

_____ Everyone should receive cultural training from the corporate university, but skills can be learned on the job.

_____ The corporate university should have a corporatewide charter.

_____ The corporate university should only focus on corporate-level activities and not have any direct impact on individual product divisions.

_____ Senior-level management can benefit from formal education and development, but others in the organization can learn on the job.

_____ The business units can decide for themselves who needs development and they can pay for it themselves, as well.

_____ The corporate university should be responsible only for management or leadership development.

_____ The corporate university should dictate some common curriculums across the corporation.

_____ Employees should go to external universities on their own time and get tuition reimbursement. Development is not a corporate responsibility.

_____ Employee development is a big expense and most employees will leave after we have invested money in their training.

Now, review the statements you have chosen. Are those you have checked complementary or contradictory assumptions? For example, if you have checked that the corporate university should have a corporatewide charter and that some curriculums should be common across the organization, you have a set of complementary and self-strengthening statements. However, if you checked off that everyone should get training and that the corporate university should be for managers only, then there is a major contradiction.

You should get a small team of people together to review these statements and even add new ones. These assumptions are significant because if you have chosen ones that are not generally agreed on, it will be very difficult to move forward.

How you and your leadership answer these questions will determine whether you can successfully create a corporate university and, if so, whom it should serve. Many corporate universities fail at this stage and never get majority agreement and senior-level management support for their chosen scope and intended audience. Successful corporate universities such as those at General Electric and McDonald's have a crystal clear, well-defined set of stakeholders, and no one questions who gets trained.

Operating Principles

People often do not think about the consequences of their assumptions and principles and how they are to be implemented in the corporate university. For example, if you choose to create a corporate university focused on leadership and management, what impact will this have on productivity of hourly workers?

The corporate university makes a statement to and about the whole company. It publicly underlines who is considered the most valuable and ~~you~~ are willing to invest.

~~st~~ organizations these operating principles are ~~et~~ if you were to try to put together a corporate ~~antly~~ counter to one of these unwritten assump~~ess~~ are going to be limited. Like an architect of a corporate university has to understand the prin~~stakeholders. You would not be a successful archi~~ a classical New England home for lovers of modern a palace for an ordinary citizen. You have to under~~the university will operate in and have a sense for~~ want and what will be credible to everyone.

Scope

Scope is also a credibility issue. Your success in large part depends on being able to "right size" the corporate university. Often, organizations have a scope that exceeds their reach. They do not have the financial resources or staff to follow through. Sometimes they do not have the expertise. For example, a corporate university consisting of an organization of development and training professionals will fail if it attempts to advise senior leadership on new strategic directions. These people most likely do not have the operational or practical experience to be seen as credible.

Another pitfall is deciding on a scope that is unlikely to be funded or resourced. Paula, in our opening example, did not understand the level of resources that the organization was willing to provide. In Chapter Seven, we will look more deeply at the issue of funding, which is an ongoing consideration at every step.

Early Planning

As we will explore in the next chapter, it is critical to identify your governance committee and get buy-in and direction before moving forward. In the next chapter, you will identify your key players through creation of a governance committee. Once you have strategy and governance in place, you can finalize your assessment of scope and operating principles. At this point, you can do some prework with your trusted early advisors.

You can begin with a small planning committee of people who will be your trusted advisors and inside support group. You can take the answers from Exercise 3.1 and engage your planning committee in a critical conversation with the intent to come to a clear decision, agree, and commit to a certain set of operating principles and scope. Later you will take these ideas to the full governance committee for additional refinement so that they can recommend and obtain the right level of resources.

Again, the process of creating a corporate university does not move in a straight line. Rather, it involves continual looping back to original ideas and refinement of decisions as new data and input arrive. Looking back at the first chapter, reconsider the value proposition of your corporate university. Do your assumptions about scope fit with those? What is the logic behind your vision of the scope and operating principles as they align with your strategy?

Often, planning committees will not treat the discussion of operating principles seriously. They will assume they know without really engaging in conversation. You can overcome this barrier by putting in place a process that will allow you to get to true dialog about these issues. People may think they already agree, but it will be up to you to push the conversation deeper. For example, even if everyone agrees that the corporate university should focus on management development, you still need to look at scope. Are you going to provide development for all management? Are you including the senior level of management? Or is your focus going to be on midlevel managers? What is the priority and what is the logic?

These conversations about scope and operating principles ultimately affect the entire organization. Typically, little thought is given as to how the corporate university's scope is communicated to others. Important questions for your governance committee to address include

- What will be the effect on the morale of the rest of the organization?

- How is this corporate university's charter going to be received?

- What preparation or messages can be put together to help make your chosen direction acceptable throughout the organization?

The action steps of defining your scope and operating principles will be challenging. Your stakeholders—from human resources and the training department to managers and employees—assume that everyone else has similar assumptions about who should receive training. Leading the critical conversations about scope and operating principles can be enlightening and prevent unfulfilled expectations while opening a wider path to the success of your corporate university.

Action Steps

Using Template 3.1, work first with your trusted advisors and then with the governance committee to answer these questions:

- If you were to be perceived as having a strong impact on the organization, upon whom would you have to concentrate your development efforts?

- Which group of employees would benefit the most?

- Where is senior management's concern and pain?

- Is there a group of people whose successful development would provide the corporate university with an early win?

- Are there internal talent needs the corporate university could address and thereby lower recruiting costs?

- Has your succession planning process identified gaps that development could fill?

Your answers to these questions will help you determine:

- *Stakeholders.* Who really cares about these issues and could have an affect on your decisions?

- *Recipients.* Who is going to be served?

- *Scope.* What levels and geographies will be served?

Conclusion

From this chapter you now have a deeper understanding of how important it is to make explicit what is often assumed and unspoken. You should have some tools and skills to help you articulate who your most important stakeholders are and for making sure they are included in your planning and development stages. Without this knowledge, you are likely to meet with opposition, uncertainty, and even suspicion about your ultimate motivation. Likewise, you are now able to better uncover the operating principles that executives use to make decisions about what is important or valuable to the organization.

TEMPLATE 3.1

Defining Scope

Defining Scope

Management's Concerns/Pains:

Key Stakeholders:

Internal Talent Needs:

Geographic Scope:

Succession Planning Needs:

Groups Whose Success Will Have the Greatest Impact:

Designed by Eileen Clegg

Chapter 4

Governance
Who Decides What?

EVERY CORPORATE UNIVERSITY has a governance body of some sort, even if it is only the CEO. However, is this governance effective, and does it help or hinder your ability to add value to your organization? You can spend a whole lot of time and energy working with people who are not empowered to give you the resources and direction you need.

One major American organization has had a corporate university for a number of years, but it has gone through many changes in direction and is generally not considered to be highly effective. One of the reasons for this is a very unclear original charter. The original idea was to educate external customers on how to use the products they made. Over time, employees and managers were included, although there was no specific charter to do this. There was no governance committee in place, and the training department more or less went where demand took them. This led to a profitable, but unfocused, corporate university that has suffered significantly during the latest economic downturn and suffers from mixed internal credibility. Some managers feel it is doing a good job, while others feel that it is a waste of time. It is hard to prove any specific return on the investment but equally hard to prove that there has been no return. This is the classic paradox of many corporate universities and training organizations. But a clearer, stronger governance committee could have helped by clearly defining and supporting a specific agenda and strategic direction, and even by articulating the expected outcomes.

At Edwards Lifesciences, both the CEO and the executive vice president for human resources realized there was a need to build leadership excellence among midlevel managers of the organization. One of the executive directors of the organization agreed to act as a member of a planning committee that would lay out the charter and the content for a corporate university. Included on this team were the director of training and development, a number of senior-level line managers, and two other executives. Over a series of several months, this committee engaged in vigorous discussion and debate about the operating principles, goals, scope, and actual content that should be delivered. The outcomes were reviewed by the entire executive leadership team for their comments, and eventually a clear scope and charter were approved. The program has been operating successfully for more than a year, has been resourced fully, and will continue to be offered in the future.

Direction and focus are critical. Corporate universities that have vaguely defined missions and overly broad charters are rarely successful. This chapter takes you through the process of setting up a formal structure to provide strategic guidance and approval for your actions and also to give you influence over resource levels.

The Importance of Governance

In every organization, there is a person or group of people who make the decisions, not just about what kind of training and development you will be offering, but also about how your work aligns with the organization. It is important in the early stages of planning a corporate university that you put together a governance or planning team to help you choose the right strategic focus. You need to decide who in the organization is going to be the final decision maker on your strategy, your scope, your customers, your stakeholders, and your resources. All too often those who are key influencers are never identified or are ignored in the process of setting up a corporate university. Yet these are the people who have the power over whether you survive or fail.

The governing body sets the direction for the corporate university, gives final approval for the strategic direction of the corporate university, evaluates its success, and helps to communicate its achievements internally and externally. Although the governance body is not necessarily whom the corporate university staff reports to, it does have a direct influence on the corporate university's long-term success. Those on the governing body should be dedicated to the concept, available for input, and willing to champion the corporate university to the rest of the corporation's management and employees.

Choosing your governing committee is a strategic decision with consequences that will affect how well you can execute. Engaging your governing committee is key to effectiveness. More than a few corporate universities have put together boards made up of people with good reputations, clear opinions, and corporate clout only to never reap any benefit. Usually this occurs because the corporate university's management team does not know how to use the board well.

The Right Balance

It is important that no critical stakeholder is left out of the process. At the same time, you will need to make sure the committee is not so large that it gets bogged down in bureaucracy and procedure. The governance committee needs to be small (not more than seven people), high-level, and strategic. You may later establish subcommittees to focus on implementation features, such as curriculum or staff selection. For example, one company's training focused on disseminating and improving skill levels of engineering employees. They had a separate engineering council that consisted of two highly respected engineering gurus, an engineering director, and a first-line engineering manager who hired college graduates and engineers with only a few years' experience. This group provided a clear picture of engineering needs and helped training stay relevant.

In the beginning, however, you will need to identify the key players in the organization who can guide, support, and fund your mission. You may not find all the key players inside. Sometimes a corporate university benefits from representation outside the corporation. For example, someone from a university or a leading-edge learning company can add an important perspective. It may allow the corporate university access to research and provide an avenue to influence university curriculum to the company's benefit.

Although it is unwise to overlook key players in establishing governance, it also is unwise to try and bring in too many people. As you select your governance committee, keep in mind these pitfalls:

1. Too many members—select only those who are key decision makers and keep the committee no more than seven people.

2. A committee that spends its time philosophizing on the nature of training and not staying focused on what the company needs.

3. Only having HR and training people governing the corporate university; instead you need a cross-section of people with credibility and business knowledge.

Begin to determine who will serve on your governance board by convening the design team and completing Exercise 4.1 on page 44. After holding another meeting with a cross-functional group from the organization (see the exercise instructions), the design team should meet again to discuss the results and to fill in Template 4.1.

EXERCISE 4.1

Selecting a Governance Board

Your design team should answer the questions below. These will help decide who to involve in the governance process. Once you have gone through the questions, meet with a small, cross-functional group of internal people who are knowledgeable about your organization and familiar with your plans for the corporate university. Enlist them to look over the initial slate of potential members for the governance committee and ask them to suggest other names or recommend names to be removed. The goal is to identify everyone who could help you put the corporate university into action and all of those who might not be as supportive. Remember, one of the best ways to work with those who disagree with you is to include them in the decision and design process.

Was the CEO the originator of the corporate university idea or concept?   YES   NO

If not, how important is it to have him or her as part of your governance team?

1	2	3	4	5
Essential				Optional

If yes, who would he or she want on this governance committee? List at least three or four.

_____

_____

_____

_____

List a few others who are influential and provide a cross-functional view of the organization.

_____

_____

_____

_____

Who is needed to provide approval for expenditures?

_____

_____

Who has the most knowledge of the company's strategy and future direction?

_____

_____

Who else needs to be included in order to ensure that the corporate university is not politically compromised?

_____

_____

Who are people outside the corporation who might add value to your governing body?

_____

_____

Who are key subject matter experts inside your organization that need to be included?

_____

_____

Defining Your Governance Board

Defining Your Governance Board

Who would the CEO want on the governance team?

The ideal governance team short list:

Influential people with a cross-functional view of the company:

Who from outside the organization would add value?

Who will provide approval for expenditures?

Who has the most knowledge of the company's strategy and future direction?

Who else needs to be included to make sure the Corporate University is not politically compromised?

Key subject matter experts inside the organization:

Designed by Eileen Clegg

Rallying of the Committee

Once you have identified the people you want to be on your governance board, you are ready to extend the invitation. When invited to participate in these committees, people usually are more than willing to participate. Almost everybody believes there is potential value in ongoing development and education. Rest assured that most people will say "yes" to your offer of involvement. Follow your instincts about whom to select first. Especially if you have powerful people already on board, others will follow.

The invitation should set the stage for success. It needs to be a carefully written letter that explains the rationale or business case for creating the corporate university and its intended goals, objectives, and benefits to the organization. Explain why they have been invited to participate and what is expected from them. Also, provide a general outline of the purpose and scope of the governance committee, even though this may change as you get into actual meetings and better define and understand the expected outcomes. This invitation and any subsequent communication should detail the expected time commitments, amount of work expected outside of the committee meetings, and how long they are expected to be a member of the advisory board. You may wish to limit terms to one year. This will make it much easier to invite less productive and helpful members to retire and invite new ones to join.

Relationship Building

Often, directors of corporate universities will avoid tapping the shoulders of key leaders in the organization because they want to avoid conflicts between different people's opinions about the direction, focus, and scope. This is a legitimate concern. It is a challenge to harness positive energy of powerful people who have diverse opinions.

The major challenge is to bring finesse and a long view into the interactions with your governing board. You will want to have positive, critical conversations that result in useful outcomes. Facilitation is the key. Have a process and action plan that can focus groups on the issues and encourage them to reach consensus. This is particularly important at this juncture as you are creating your support team and you want them to be communicating and feeling heard, as well as engaged and all aligned. This cannot be overemphasized.

Action Steps

Make sure your CEO agrees that the people you have chosen for the governance committee are the right ones—those he or she respects and to whom he or she will listen. It is even better if the CEO has a hand in picking the members and is also a member.

Although the governance board should meet regularly during the year, it is wise to get started with two meetings, separated by some time. This will help members engage in the critical conversations that will lay the foundation for the growth and success of the corporate university. Generally, two half-day meetings separated by a few weeks is adequate, but you may decide to have meetings that are more frequent.

Prepare a detailed agenda and make sure members know the contributions expected from them. Build in enough time for exploring issues and for members to get to know one another. It may be best to follow the meeting with dinner or have a lunch with plenty of opportunity for informal conversation.

At the first meeting, present your concept and ideas, your first cuts on operating principles and strategic direction. Post your completed templates from Chapters Two and Three and engage the group in a conversation about them. Have a blank copy of the templates posted as well, and make changes suggested by the members. Have a visual facilitator—someone who is trained in recording meetings publicly by using graphic techniques and large sheets of paper—lead you through a brainstorming session to refine and expand or change your ideas. You can also ask the committee members to consider their various roles and responsibilities, which can be recorded on Template 4.2.

Let a few weeks pass between each of the half-day meetings. Use this time to talk to each member individually and to allow him or her time to think through what has been discussed. Collect opinions, objections, concerns, and positives to present at the next group meeting.

At the second meeting, bring up the things you have heard from members, solicit their thoughts, and work to come to a final agreement on operating principles and strategic direction. The end product of these first series of meetings is agreement on a working vision and strategy for the corporate university, along with at least the beginnings of an implementation roadmap.

TEMPLATE 4.2

Governance: Roles and Responsibilities

Governance: Roles and Responsibilities

Role:

Responsibilities:

Role:

Role:

Responsibilities:

Role:

Responsibilities:

Role:

Responsibilities:

Designed by Eileen Clegg

Conclusion

Efficiency and good communication are dramatically enhanced by the effort to clarify the roles and responsibilities of the governance committee. You can have many players as long as they understand their part in reaching the goal. It will be an ongoing challenge to keep everyone focused and inspired about his or her roles. Again, digitizing and circulating the completed template on governance roles and responsibilities will be helpful in reminding people of their initial agreements. As the leader, it will also be incumbent on you to keep in mind the personalities of those involved, provide them feedback, and assign duties based on their individual motivations. Governance, like most aspects of creating a corporate university, may change as the strategy and focus of your corporate university evolves. However, for now it is important to have the continuity of a stable, well-informed leadership team as you move forward.

Chapter 5
Organizing the Corporate University

PEOPLE SPEND a lot of time talking about the structure of the corporate university, yet this should be simple: the structure should be a reflection of strategic intent and the needs of the organization.

A small company with about 1,800 employees developed a corporate university with a completely decentralized structure. Each manufacturing unit had its own training function, and the corporate university provided space and whatever training they could convince the units to pay for. Each unit did exactly what it wanted, with no commonality. There was no integration of knowledge, no sharing except incidentally. The corporate university had no brand and little identity, and everyone was confused about what it did and why it even existed. Obviously, within a short time it ceased to exist.

When deciding how to organize, one Fortune 500 company's corporate university immediately uncovered several critical issues. The company had factories in six countries and faced the need to deliver content in five languages. The members of the governance committee disagreed on who should receive management development, as management levels were inconsistent from country to country. There were also philosophical differences over the use of 360-degree feedback tools. The dilemma the committee faced was how to organize itself to meet all the demands. The final resolution was to adopt a partially decentralized structure with a strong corporate core, but also with strong foundations within each country. In effect, they agreed on a federal structure with certain things being common yet with a great deal of independence for each country.

Once the corporate university has direction and a mission, it needs to have the appropriate structure to enable it to achieve the mission. Having a structure that is not well aligned with the mission can cause uncertainty, confusion, and even derail the university entirely. This chapter discusses various ways corporate universities can be organized and lays out some guidelines for which structure to choose.

Different Models

There are three basic structural models that are commonly used for corporate universities: centralized, decentralized, or federal.

The Centralized Model

All activities and people involved in developing and delivering learning and all those involved in capturing and disseminating knowledge report to a single person. This is a very effective model when an organization is small or when there is a need to vigorously drive programs and initiatives throughout the firm. Often large organizations use this structure to get things started, and then gradually give way to a different model that allows for more local autonomy. For success, the leader of a centralized corporate university must have high credibility, be able to offer clear direction and strategy, and have enough vision to keep the staff and organization engaged.

This model is common in organizations of fewer than 2,000 employees and where there is only a single office or a handful of small offices closely tied to the corporate headquarters. It allows for efficient decision making and makes tracking of costs and service easier. Often organizations with this structure have very small training departments made up of just one or two people who leverage external resources for development and delivery. The centralized model is also often found in larger organizations where there is a tightly defined purpose for the corporate university, or when there is a need for rapid change and no time for group process. The Leadership Institute at General Electric is charted by its CEO, and he has closely controlled and helped craft its leadership curriculum.

In summary, this model is well suited when

- Training departments are small (one or two people).
- The organization has fewer than 2,000 employees.
- The charter is narrow and tightly defined.
- There is a need for rapid change.

The Decentralized Model

In this model, there is no controlling central organization or central direction. The corporate unit, if it exists, is usually just another training function similar to the others that may exist. It may have a special charter to deliver leadership development, for example, act as the clearinghouse for vendors, or coordinate the activities of senior management around learning. The central group might be responsible for senior leadership off-sites and other similar activities, and it may offer programs to the business units, often for a fee.

But the difference is that each function or branch has complete freedom to use these services or develop and deliver its own curricula. The division or branch controls content, timing, and cost. If an organization has independent business units, strong general managers, and needs flexibility in how it deals with different functions or parts of the firm, this model can work. Often global organizations inadvertently adopt this structure because it minimizes having to deal with the cultural and local differences such organizations face. However, the decentralized model is not best for achieving cost efficiencies or consistency in content. Its primary benefit is to put the control of development closest to the learner, which can mean that content is more current, more likely to be immediately relevant, and often available faster than in other models.

This model is often found in midsized to large organizations that have grown rapidly, or that are conglomerates with divisions that are virtually independent organizations and where there is a strong general manager.

In summary, this model can work when

- There are profit centers with general managers who control other parts of their business independently of corporate.

- The organization is a conglomerate and there is little in common between divisions.

- The organization is widely dispersed globally with very different local needs.

The Federal Model

This structure consists of a strong central group that influences, coordinates, and ties together all disparate training functions worldwide. However, it does not have direct ownership or control over the different training functions that exist. Each one, in effect, chooses to delegate some of its authority to the central or corporate group for the sake of consistency and effectiveness. The corporate group (working collaboratively with the business unit's university divisions) gets agreement on a common strategy, develops key curricula, provides information systems support, and funds key programs. However, business units are allowed a great deal of local autonomy and can develop courses that meet local needs without permission from the central unit.

In the federal model, the central group should be responsible for

1. Co-creating and communicating a central strategy that, through a process of consensus building, is acceptable to all the divisions and branches

2. Developing a core curriculum for leadership and management that provides a consistent leadership philosophy and approach

3. Providing a common technology platform for tracking, delivering, and reporting educational and development activities

4. Deciding on a core set of common metrics that all divisions and branches track and report

5. Developing classes, developing curriculums, or undertaking special projects as jointly decided on by the various divisions

This model allows the divisions to respond quickly to local needs and provide relevant and cost-effective solutions quickly without sacrificing the common elements that make for harmonious relationships and overall organization success.

This model is ideally suited for large, multinational organizations or any organization with numerous branches or divisions of a sufficient size (usually more than 1,000 employees) to support independent development activities. In selecting the federal model, National Semiconductor University reflected its global position as an organization with branches in many parts of the world that demanded autonomy and flexibility in developing their workers. The central organization's function became one of setting standards and developing and implementing a common curriculum.

In summary, this model works well when

- Your organization is very large and dispersed with common needs.
- There is already a level of duplication of services or curriculums that need merging or coordinating.
- Your organization is global and needs a common core but lots of local flexibility.

Table 5.1 provides a summary of the three models.

TABLE 5.1

Characteristics of Each Model of Corporate University

Type	Characteristics	Pros, Cons, Comments
Federal	Core provides: Common strategic direction Common operating standards Funding for selected programs Common systems and processes Common IT infrastructure Core curricula Common set of metrics Training for CU staff Individual units provide: All other desired development Local strategy Individual development programs Collaborative arrangement with local colleges and universities	Good compromise between central and decentralized types. However, does take autonomy from business unit groups. Builds business unit responsibility—makes them decide what is really important for them to control. Provides consistency in development from unit to unit and allows for more flexible succession planning.
Centralized	All direction comes from a center. All training and development is consistent everywhere in the organization. Good for getting things implemented fast. Provides direction in times of turmoil.	Does not allow units any autonomy and may lead to inappropriate programs for some of those units. Leaves no freedom to units. Builds an overreliance on corporate resources. Lets managers think that training and development are "free."
Decentralized	Everybody does their own thing. No one at the corporate level has any overall say or can provide direction, unless asked.	Allows units total autonomy and responsibility for training and development. May penalize employees in units that offer little or no training. Does not ensure a strong talent development process for succession planning. Primary benefit is autonomy. Many negatives.

Hybrid Model

In addition to the three main models, variations, or hybrid models, are also possible. Some organizations have developed corporate universities that combine elements. For example, a centrally organized corporate university may have one function that is decentralized, although all the others are under the corporate university banner. Several companies have centralized leadership development, safety and technical training, employee orientation or on-boarding, and other development functions but have left sales training independent. This type of variation occurs when a functional area is already doing a good job at developing its employees or when the functional head is politically strong and does not want to be part of a more centralized function. In each case you will have to make a decision about how much energy and time you will use trying to bring all the various existent development functions under the corporate university. Often it is better, and easier, to let the merger of departments happen slowly over time.

Other examples of these hybrid corporate universities include those that have centralized development in their home country but have left the international development decentralized. In other organizations, international factories or offices may join into regional development networks while the corporate headquarters remains focused domestically.

Safety and operator training are often excluded from the corporate university and left entirely up to operations groups to develop and deliver.

Combinations of types are common and in no way indicate that the corporate university is ineffective or weak. The important point is that the corporate university should be seen as delivering bottom-line value and helping the organization achieve its business goals.

The Design Team can use Exercise 5.1 on page 56 to start thinking about the best structure for the organization's corporate university.

How to Decide

If your organization is in trouble or needs to change strategic direction quickly, then the centralized model is effective. With that model, you can marshal resources quickly and get people moving without a lot of discussion and consensus building. If you are a small- to medium-sized organization located entirely within the United States with fewer than five branches, the most effective structure will also likely be a centralized model. There will be a single source from which all development, training, and knowledge management occurs.

EXERCISE 5.1

Choosing a Structure

Answers to these questions will help give you a sense for which structure will enhance your chances of success. After you complete this exercise, read the chapter section How to Decide.

How many employees work in your organization?

1–1,000	1,001–3,000	3,001–10,000	More than 10,000
Small	Medium	Large	Gigantic

How many branches are there in the United States?

Only 1 (headquarters)   2–4   5 or more

Is your charter or focus narrow and tightly defined?

Do you have common needs for certain types of training?

Is there a history or experience with shared services and responsibilities?

How many significant offices or factories do you have in other countries?

None   1–4   5 or more

How many different languages are spoken in your company?

Only 1 primary   2 primary (both widely spoken)   Many

What is your chosen strategic approach (see Chapter Two)?

_____ Change management focus

_____ Strategic or business focus

_____ Skill and development focus

_____ External customer focus

_____ Research

How is your organization structured?

_____ Centralized

_____ Business units with general managers

Is your organization in a hurry to implement new curricula?

However, if your company has many branches within your country, or has a skill and development strategic focus, you could consider a federal structural model. This model allows both control and flexibility and offers a very nice compromise between no freedom and total freedom (which often means chaos). If you are a multinational company where multiple languages are spoken and with many offices or factories and branches in other countries, probably the most effective model would be a version of the federal model. The decentralized model does not provide the common elements and collaboration that allow for greater efficiencies.

If you work in a large organization that is globally dispersed with highly autonomous leaders, the decentralized model is almost inevitable, although if there are common needs (for example, leadership development, or a common culture and philosophy), then it may be possible to implement the federal model.

Ideally, your corporate university structure should map to your overall corporate structure. If your corporation is diverse, with units that operate with autonomy, then the decentralized or federal models will make the most sense because they provide those same characteristics.

We have described pure, textbook-like structures, but in the real world, as you have seen in the examples of combined and hybrid corporate universities described above, there are many variations of these structures. We hope that by using these ideal models initially in your planning, you can better choose a structure that will let you deliver what the organization needs as efficiently as you can.

Sharing the Decision: The Role of the Governance Committee

It should be clear from your knowledge and what you've read above which structure would be the most likely to help you accomplish your objectives and goals. However, this choice needs to be examined by the governance committee members and agreed to by them, and the appropriate resources have to be available. When discussing your model with your governance committee, consider the following.

Resources

In the federal and decentralized models, there is an assumption that each business unit will offer some form of training to its employees. If the business unit does not provide the resources for this, employees may be short-changed.

Fairness and Employee Morale

The structure could have an impact on employee morale as some employees find themselves without development opportunities whereas others, in different business units, have what they need. If one of the divisions decides not to implement the corporate university because of financial or other reasons, there will be consequences you may have to face.

The Governance Issue

As the structure is determined, the governance committee will have to take a stance on these issues:

- What is the governance decision going to be if one or more branches of an organization decide not to participate?
- How will the organization ensure fairness?
- How will funding be handled?

In the end, the answers to these questions will tell everyone how important the corporate university is to your top leadership. This is where governance becomes pivotal. For example, at National Semiconductor University, when the different units saw how important education was to the CEO, even unmotivated unit management committed resources. At these junctures, a strong governance committee and CEO support really pay off and become pivotal to putting the corporate university in place.

Form reflects function. Therefore, your structure has to support your success. Many organizations have structures that work against them. By thinking the question of structure through carefully with your governance committee, you will not only start successfully but also sustain your success.

Action Steps

While meeting with the governance committee, examine the different models for your corporate university. Use this meeting as an opportunity to understand the needs of top leadership and probe into motivations. Be crystal clear what the governance committee expects from the corporate university and make sure this is what you can deliver.

Using Template 5.1, list the pros and cons you see for your organization around each model. Discuss variations or combinations of these models that might be more appropriate in your situation. List the objections you might hear from the business units about each structure. Discuss how to overcome resource and access issues.

TEMPLATE 5.1

Structure of Your Corporate University

Structure of Your Corporate University

Centralized Model

Pros:

Cons:

Resources:

Access:

Decentralized Model

Pros:

Cons:

Resources:

Access:

Federal Model

Pros:

Cons:

Resources:

Access:

Hybrid Model

Pros:

Cons:

Resources:

Access:

Designed by Eileen Clegg

Tentatively decide on a working structural model that the committee feels will be most effective in achieving strategic objectives and that best matches the organization's existing structure. Choosing a collaborative model within a highly controlled organization will probably not be successful, and vice versa.

Conclusion

In this chapter, you have seen how various organizational factors influence the selection of one of the three basic structural models. The choice of a structure should follow naturally from your strategic direction and from the work that you have undertaken with your governance committee, and through the planning that has led you to this point.

It is very important to understand that no structure will automatically ensure success. A structure is at best a framework for decision making and organizing how work gets done, yet the interactions between people and the corporate culture all play a major part in whether or not the corporate university is successful. What we are trying to stress throughout this book is the need for alignment and harmony between all the various subsystems that make up the corporate university. In the next chapter, we begin to look at the skills and competencies of the staff that will co-create and implement the strategic direction you have adopted through this structure.

Chapter 6

Staffing the Corporate University

BUILDING A STAFF, identifying the kinds of people you need, and then finding and developing them is the ultimate challenge of the corporate university leadership. The only way to do this is by having a systematic plan and your own vision of what can be.

One of the questions always asked about staffing a corporate university is how many staff there should be. Of course, there is no simple answer to that. Staffing levels need to follow the strategic approach of the university and fit the culture and size of the organization. One organization with more than 30,000 employees scattered in fourteen countries has a very small central corporate university staff made up of a handful of program managers who leverage external resources. The entire central staff is eleven people. Each has an area of responsibility such as leadership development or technical training. They find vendors to develop and deliver the training and use other employees as subject matter experts. There is a focus on teaching managers to teach and to move basic skills training to e-learning. Costs are well controlled and easily justified, and the productivity levels are high.

Another organization, also with about 30,000 employees and a narrower global presence, was staffed very differently. It had at one time more than a hundred people in a variety of specialties, including instructional designers, multimedia and graphics experts, standup trainers, administrators, and measurement experts. They produced hundreds of courses, often before any need had been expressed. The director of this corporate university told me that he worried most about keeping the instructional designers busy! As might be expected, when management began to scrutinize the university, it was impossible to justify the number of people. There were layoffs and many other cuts as the university repositioned itself. A poorly thought-out staffing model can be devastating.

Even with the best strategy, mission, structure, and governance board possible, execution is completely dependent on the caliber of the people who work in the corporate university. Choosing the right people—those who understand the mission and have the skills and motivation to help achieve it—is the most important step in the development of the corporate university. This chapter discusses the skills that may be needed, how to determine what skills your current or future staff need to have, and how to make sure the skills are compatible with the strategic direction and structure of the university and the delivery methods you will use.

The Roles of the Corporate University Staff

After you have determined the strategic orientation, scope, and structure of your corporate university, you can begin to think about how to staff the corporate university. For each position, the corporate university leadership will have to ask itself how the position adds value to the organization. People add value to organizations in four ways: (1) making specific items or providing needed services, (2) buying or selling products or services, (3) creating or inventing new products or services, or (4) coordinating the performance of other employees. Of course, most of us do some of each of these in our work, but one is usually dominant over the others. For example, a manager has to influence and sell and often even provides a service, but typically the coordination function consumes most of a manager's time.

Employees whose primary function is to make a product or deliver a service often are called production workers, assemblers, operators, or consultants or have titles that suggest that they directly touch the product or service and help shape and create it. These are the producers of an organization and are essential to success.

Other employees may focus on influencing others to buy the product or on actually selling the product to customers. Whether a person is involved in marketing, advertising, product design and usability, or goes out and does face-to-face selling, he or she is part of this category of employee that we call sellers.

A third category of employees develops, designs, and invents the products or services that are sold. These employees may be located in research and development departments; they may do research, conduct surveys, or find information that will be useful in designing a new service or product. These people are called inventors.

And a fourth type of employee can be called a coordinator—someone who directs and manages the activities of other people. In the corporate world, these are usually supervisors, managers, directors, or vice presidents, but they could also be project managers or other employees who coordinate work and keep the organization and its people focused and moving in a common direction.

In every corporate university, there are people who fill these various roles. Some employees in the corporate university create new courses, determine learning needs, and measure skill gaps. Others design training materials or deliver that training in the classroom or by e-learning. Others market the corporate university's capabilities and perhaps sell development services within the organization. And, of course, a few employees coordinate and manage all of this.

Employees in the corporate university may add value in diverse ways, but more than likely one of these value types dominate. If the primary needs will involve developing extensive new curriculums, then the corporate university will need people capable of that development. If the need is more focused on organizing what exists and providing smoother delivery processes, then those employees who can organize and manage may be more critical at first. There may be a need to drive extensive change through the organization or to build a more competent leadership team. Using the strategy you have developed, and working with the governance committee, you should be able to decide, at least in a preliminary manner, what the mix of the general types listed in Exercise 6.1 on page 64 should be.

Five Steps for Building Your Staff

Once you have determined the mix of types that will be most appropriate for your organization, there are five additional steps in the process of assessing and selecting your staff.

1. *Determine competencies.* Like everything else to do with the corporate university, staffing must be tied to your organization's strategic objectives. The competencies that you need will be dictated by the strategic approach you have chosen. Exercise 6.2 on page 65 will help you think through this step.

2. *Assess your current staff.* Once you have determined the competencies that will best serve your strategic approach, you will need to evaluate any current staff to see how well they meet these competency needs.

EXERCISE 6.1

Value-Added Role

The table below contains some commonly used titles for people who are employed in corporate universities. Place an X in the box under the column describing the value-added focus that best fits each position. Blank rows are provided for you to write in your own titles.

Job Title	Producer	Seller	Inventor	Coordinator
Trainer				
Instructional designer				
Course developer				
Administrator				
Manager/director				
e-Learning designer				
Organization development expert				
Assessment expert				
Training coordinator				
Executive coach				

EXERCISE 6.2

Determining Competencies Needed by Staff

Look back at Chapter Two and consider all four strategies for a corporate university. Although you have already determined a particular strategy for your corporate university, this exercise involves all four strategies to help you begin thinking about the importance of strategic staffing.

For each of the four types of strategy, list what you believe to be the top four competencies required of staff. We have included a partial list of possible competencies and skills to consider, but please add your own. Take a few hours and discuss these with other people, perhaps your own staff, and try to get a broad level of agreement on the competencies that fit each strategy—even if you are not going to pursue that approach. You will discover the differences and have an opportunity to, once again, confirm that your chosen strategic approach is the correct one.

Sample Competencies and Skills

Innovation	Establishing rapport with others
Verbal fluency	Focused
Creativity	Attention to detail
Multitasking	Customer relations
Strategic thinking	Stability
Problem analysis	Learning speed
Active listening	Able to build internal support
Global perspective	Persuasion
Business/functional knowledge	Ability to adapt
Coaching	Mental agility
Technical skills	Competitive knowledge
Future orientation	Adherence to standards
Appreciation of quality	

Competencies and skills needed to staff a change management focused corporate university:

_____
_____
_____

Competencies and skills needed to staff a business development focused corporate university:

_____
_____
_____

Competencies and skills needed to staff a skill and development focused corporate university:

_____
_____
_____

Competencies and skills needed to staff an external customer focused corporate university:

_____
_____
_____

3. *Conduct a gap analysis.* After comparing the competencies of your current staff to those you need, determine which competencies you have and those you don't.

4. *Choose your staffing model.* There are three staffing models—program management model, mixed model, team development model—and you can choose the one that will meet your corporate philosophy.

5. *Implement your staffing and hiring plan.* Using best practices in recruitment and staffing, go through the process of finding the best people for your corporate university.

Staff Competencies for Your Strategic Direction

Below you will find a discussion of the competencies that are useful or even necessary to execute each of the four types of corporate universities.

Change Management

If the strategic charter is change management, then the staff should be future-oriented and must understand the direction of the industry you are in, as well as the general strategic direction of your organization. Competencies these people need include an understanding of the organization development and change management process, business knowledge, verbal fluency, persuasion, and active listening skills. You may also want people with previous experience in driving a change effort or developing corporatewide communication strategies.

A staff strong in producing and coordinating may be a liability to you if this is your direction. People who have been delivering the same kinds of training or who have been in a familiar routine for some time will feel stressed and uncomfortable in the change process.

Business Development

A business development strategic direction will require a staff with some skills that are similar to those for change management. However, these people must also have an in-depth understanding of your production or service deliverables, and how your organization makes its products or delivers its service. They will also have to understand emerging technologies and service trends. Additional competencies this staff would need include a deep business knowledge, knowledge of the future direction of the industry, an ability to understand marketing challenges, and a facility in identifying parallel skills within the organization that might be useful in this new business.

Skill and Development

A staff capable of implementing a skill and development model is quite different from the staff needed to implement the two categories above. This staff is more likely to be made up of the kinds of people that we think of when we talk about teaching or learning. Examples of skills required of this staff include a deep knowledge of current manufacturing practices or service delivery practices, an appreciation for quality, low tolerance for variance from standards, attention to detail, and perhaps good stand-up training and delivery skills.

External Customer Focus

Some corporate universities are chartered with training suppliers or vendors of products, others are asked to train dealers or franchisees, and still others may by chartered to educate the end user of the product. The skills that this group needs are obviously quite different, although they still will need an in-depth knowledge of products and services. In addition, they will need to develop a strong relationship with the customer, communicate current practices clearly, develop rapport easily, and sell the organization's ideas and concepts effectively.

As you no doubt have concluded from going through these exercises and reviewing these descriptions, one staff does not fit all strategies. You will need a strong understanding of the strategic intent and direction of the organization and of the corporate university to select the most effective staff.

Assessment of Your Current Staff

Many times organizations transition from training and development departments to corporate universities and bring along the same staff. The question to consider is whether or not the current staff has the right mix of attitudes, skills, and motivation to ensure the success of the corporate university. Whether you are transferring staff or hiring a new staff, you need to make sure the people you have on board have the competencies and the skills that you need to execute the strategy. We have often seen stand-up trainers with technical expertise suddenly chartered with driving a change program through the organization. Most of the time, this does not work very well because these people do not have the expertise in change management, or the agility and basic understanding of change processes required to be successful.

You could approach assessing your current staff in a number of ways. Once you have determined the competencies you will need to move forward, list them as shown in Table 6.1, and then rate each member of your staff on the level they demonstrate for each competency. This will help you determine

TABLE 6.1

Staff Competency Assessment

Competency or Skill	Staff Member				
	Rating scale: 1 (none) to 5 (expert)				
	Charlie	Susan	Rachael	Kevin	Tom
Problem solving	3	2	3	1	2
Change management	2	2	2	1	2
Business knowledge	3	4	2	5	2
Verbal fluency	4	4	4	4	2
Sales skills	2	4	3	4	2

Competencies and skills needed to staff an external customer focused corporate university:

_____

_____

_____

which staff members are most ready to assume the new roles and responsibilities the corporate university will require.

You could also use a professional psychologist to help you determine the needed skills and then conduct interviews and testing to help rate those on your staff. You could also conduct the interviews yourself.

An additional method that some embrace is to ask each staff member to rate themselves on each competency. Most people are aware of their own skills and can do a reasonably accurate self-assessment. This is particularly true when no layoffs are planned and when the staff members will be able to get the development they need.

Your Staffing Model

There are three commonly used models for staffing a corporate university. The first step in assessing current staff, or in assessing those you are interviewing from outside, is to know which of these models is most appropriate for you. For most, the choice is clear, dictated by corporate culture, executive expectations, and the strategic direction of the corporate university. Each of the models is described below; you can use Template 6.1 to help you define the right choice for your corporate university.

TEMPLATE 6.1
Hiring Plan

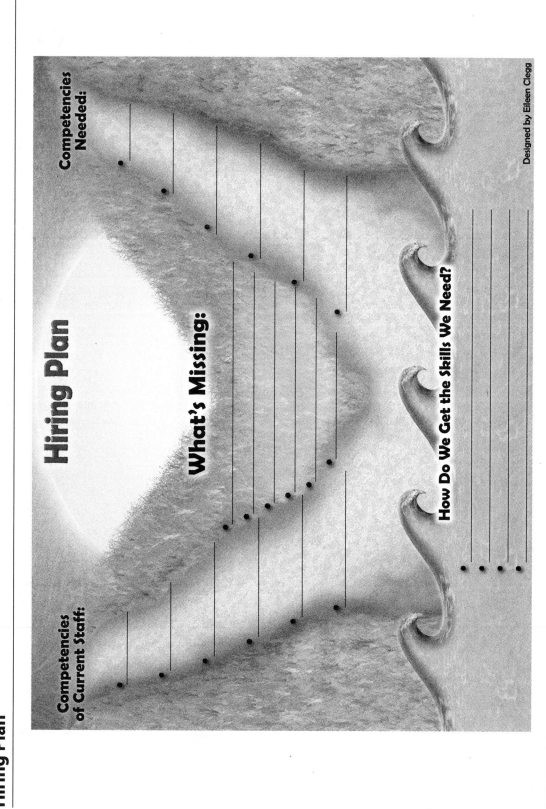

Program Management Model

Under this model, the corporate university contains a core group of employees who are primarily program managers with skills in business strategy, needs assessment, project management, and finding the right suppliers to develop and deliver learning needs. These individuals do not perform the training, but instead work with management to identify skill gaps, negotiate and manage vendors who supply the products, and assess the results. There may be an extended staff who provide technical expertise in one or more areas, perform assessment and metrics, or coordinate and administer various programs. This model is illustrated in Figure 6.1 below.

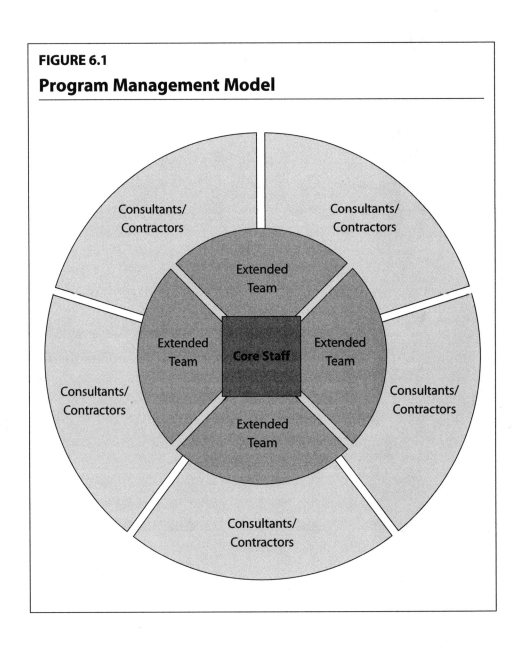

FIGURE 6.1

Program Management Model

This model is often selected when there is limited budget for expanding staff and where the corporate culture stresses lean organizations. In the age of outsourcing that we are currently in, this model is becoming popular. It reduces the direct overhead costs and keeps the internal corporate university staff small. It allows for rapid expansion of development and an equally rapid ramp down if circumstances change.

It requires a staff that can influence others, as it requires leveraging external and perhaps internal resources that are not within the direct control of the corporate university. It requires strong program management skills. It also requires people who can give feedback and engage in critical conversations with instructors, developers, and managers. The primary drawback of this model is that it becomes very difficult to quickly develop needed courses as development is outsourced, and the organization loses some control over proprietary material.

Team Development

A corporate university composed of several teams made up of a program manager, a content expert, and a delivery expert defines the second model. They work together to quickly develop and deliver a learning solution that will closely identify skill gaps. Bechtel Corporation has used this model to rapidly develop e-learning solutions for engineers scattered in more remote locations all over the globe. A team contains a video, graphics, or e-learning specialist; a content expert (who typically is on loan to the university from a business unit); an instructional designer; and a team leader or program manager.

This model is a good choice if the primary activity of the corporate university is to develop courses that require the skills of a variety of people. You can eliminate many communication problems that exist in functional organization structures by integrating the various skills into a single team. These teams tend to be very good at accomplishing specific goals quickly. However, teams like this are less effective when the tasks are varied and require agility. Larger teams can become bogged down in detail and internal issues, rather than focused on getting the task done. In addition, individuals in these teams may find that they lack variety in their daily work, often becoming in-depth experts in a narrow area, such as instructional design or video production, and thus they do not get the opportunity to develop program management skills.

Mixed Model

In the third model, the corporate university staff act as program managers most of the time. They spend time with management identifying skill gaps, and for most general needs, they find external vendors to develop and deliver any needed training. However, they also develop or customize training to meet specific internal strategic needs. For example, they might outsource all general skill development training but develop and deliver a core leadership program internally. The staff may spend 60 percent of their time performing needs assessment or procuring outside learning, and 40 percent on developing internal programs. The drawbacks of this model include the lack of time to focus on developing a single skill, and the need for highly adaptive and flexible staff. Nevertheless, it does encourage creative people to excel and provides a variety of experience.

Your Staffing Plan

Once you have determined the necessary competencies, assessed your current staffing needs, and determined your staffing model, it's time to start assembling the corporate university team. Staffing a corporate university is difficult because we typically are defining the concept as we hire. No standard profiles or stereotypes of who should staff a corporate university exist. This gives us freedom, but also pain. We have to work harder for that big payoff when we find a creative, influential wonder that will make us all look great.

The following are a few tips on assembling a great team to help you build a world-class corporate university. The first four tips should be helpful in the early stages of laying out the competencies and personalities needed to effectively staff up your function. They will also help you develop performance guidelines for existing staff and forge something different from the beginning as you move from a training and development function into a strategic corporate university.

Start with a Clear Plan

This sounds obvious, and it is, but it is almost never done. We all tend to jump into things without having a clear approach with well-understood and supported goals. The leader should assess which competencies and skills will be needed, and then sell this to upper management. Many times, a wonderful set of competencies is drafted, an extensive search conducted, and a person hired, only to be followed later by management asking, "Why did you hire that person? They aren't what I think we need." A little pre-selling of your vision and the skills you think are needed go a long way to avert this later potentially embarrassing and politically difficult situation.

It is also very useful to involve the senior management in developing the competencies and in interviewing and selecting. It is harder to criticize someone you had a hand in hiring. Take the time to benchmark other corporate universities and adopt competencies that correlate with success. Ask yourself what key traits made a particular individual successful. Ask the person's manager, if you can, why that person excels. Do your research and end up with a short, agreed-on, and supported "shopping list" of competencies and traits that you are hunting for.

Hire for Tomorrow, Not Today

Set your sights on tomorrow's needs, not on today's. What kind of skills will be needed on your corporate university staff in three years? In five?

Also, hire people who are bigger or better than the job at hand, knowing that the job will grow with their experience and acceptance in the organization. Jack Welch, former CEO at General Electric, almost always hired young but very innovative and promising university faculty members to head up the GE development function at Crotonville. Noel Tichy and Steven Kerr have headed this function and have been key contributors to our understanding of management and executive development. Their books and work have influenced many CEOs and have led Crotonville into new areas. They have contributed, without a doubt, to GE's success and its lead over all its competition. Strive to attract people who think big, broadly, and diversely.

Outsource Technical Skills; Hire for Strategic and Selling Skills

As suggested above, heavily staffing your corporate university with instructional designers, trainers, e-learning experts, and so forth is very expensive and limits your ability to react quickly to change. Today it is relatively easy to find instructional designers and content experts, and there are numerous consulting companies that can provide writing, design, and computer skills. Contractors can conduct interviews, create surveys, and tabulate data. Only good internal people, however, can do needs assessment, link development tightly to corporate objectives, and influence management and employees alike. Good staff must function as the agents of change—championing new ideas and concepts, selling new approaches and techniques, and clearly showing how all of these things lead to better bottom-line results. Don't become trapped in the web of technical expertise and find your organization focused more on its own needs than that of the customer's.

Look for Candidates in All Walks of Life

We have seen effective corporate university staff members who previously worked as line managers, academicians, trainers in other companies, lumberjacks (truly!), and Peace Corps volunteers. There is no previous career or set of experiences that necessarily makes a good contributor in a corporate university. What seems to make a difference is that the person be flexible and willing to experiment, have strong persuasive skills, and have an eclectic range of interests and hobbies. These kinds of people can imagine a different strategy or a changed environment and then help others see it too. Do not restrict your searches to narrow fields or industries.

Beat the Bushes

Now that you have established a plan and have a philosophy of hiring in hand, how do you execute? Where do you find these people? Your first instinct may be to go to your internal recruiter, an executive recruiter, or search agency. We recommend that you do your own search first. Begin by using the power of the Internet. If you have a good relationship with an internal recruiter, perhaps he or she can guide you. Nevertheless, by exploring the job boards, poking around various Web sites, and posting your needs on bulletin boards and in chat rooms, you should soon discover interesting people. In addition, use your own personal network and ask for referrals from friends. Go to conferences and seminars with a watchful eye for people who seem interesting, different, articulate, or who have contributed something worthwhile to the conference. These are the kinds of people you might be able to attract.

Dance the First Dance

You may not call the first rounds of interviews, *interviews*. Maybe you simply suggest that candidates come in for a coffee or ask them whether you can pick their brains for ideas. When you approach people on this basis, you can see how they think and what excites them. They are not "interviewing," so they are probably more natural and unaffected.

At this point, if the people you have spoken with all seem about right for the job, or if most of them do not meet your criteria, perhaps you need to refine your list of competencies. Maybe it is too narrow or too broad, or maybe you have uncovered some other competencies that are more appropriate. Remain flexible. Always keep adapting your needs to the situations you face internally and the competencies you need to the types of people you are interviewing. The goal is to find a set of criteria that are defined enough to give you a competent employee, yet not so narrowly defined that they limit your choices.

Conduct a Two-Hatted Interview

The next step is to interview a short list of people for the position you have. Here, you must put on two hats, each of which is complex and difficult to wear well. Hat number one is that of salesperson and influencer. Can you make the position you have seem like the best opportunity possible? Can you make the candidate excited? As Dr. John Sullivan of San Francisco State University says, "You have to WOW them." By this, he means make the job seem special, a real career-enhancing step, and a move up.

The second hat you wear is that of prober, analyzer, and interviewer. Does this person have the skills and competencies you already identified? This is where a large percentage of us fail. We do not probe. We look for our own likeness. We are as easily influenced by the candidate as the candidate is by us. We see what we want to see, not what really is.

If possible, it is always advantageous to see the candidate's work before you make an offer. Many progressive hiring managers are using their networks to find out how others within the candidate's current company perceive him or her. These hiring managers often ask for work samples or evidence of the kinds of work the candidate produces. Do not be afraid to ask for these things—they can make the difference between the great hire and the great disaster.

Close Quickly

The final step is to get consensus from your own team and from any others who will be working with or who will depend on this person, and then make a quick decision and offer. Many candidates are lost by a slow decision-making process. Candidates may have multiple offers and will not wait for yours. Speed is a real differentiator in the labor market.

Reconsider When It's Not Working

What do you do if you still haven't found the right person? If you have made a real effort to work your resources and are still empty handed, consider whether you are asking for too much. Does this person exist anywhere? Are you sure? Can you cite an example or two? We all can be unreasonable at times and not appreciate the fact that someone with 80 percent of what we want may be adequate.

If you are sure you are being realistic, then consider using a recruiting agency. The positive side is that recruiters are highly motivated to find a candidate, and many have extensive resources and contacts that may unearth someone you could not. The downside is that they can never know what you are looking for as well as you do, and they are usually quite expensive. Fees can run up to 30 percent or more of the candidate's base salary.

Outsource with Care

In some cases, you may simply decide to outsource a great deal of what may have otherwise been done internally. Whether using training suppliers for development or delivery, the key to success is a good working partnership. When selecting and managing suppliers, consider the following:

- Does the supplier have values similar to yours?
- Do they have experience, not only in their field of expertise, but in working with your industry?
- Have you talked to others who have used their products?
- Have you clarified objectives, clients, evaluation, milestones, and fees?
- Are periodic reviews established?
- Do you have a plan for what to do if the relationship is not working?

Conclusion

Staffing the corporate university is a major undertaking and should be executed with a great deal of thought. Whatever you accomplish, it will be because of the team you have assembled. Be sure you choose a staffing model that is sustainable, fits your strategic approach, and makes good sense for your organization. Costs of staff will be your single largest budget line item. The staff's relationship with the rest of the organization will be your single most important point of connection. Now that you have identified your staffing model, you will be ready to move into decisions about how your corporate university should be funded, the subject of Chapter Seven.

Chapter 7

Funding the Corporate University

THERE ARE THREE primary ways that corporate universities are funded: by corporate allocation, by partial or full recovery, or by operation as a profit center.

The corporate university at a company of 4,000 employees located entirely in the United States, although spread over three states, receives all of its funding directly from corporate allocations. This made the job of the director of the university very easy when budgeting time came around. She asked for a certain amount, primarily based on some needs analysis she did and on past budgets, and then received whatever the CFO approved. Most of the time, this was sufficient to provide a lot of training and support a staff of more than thirty trainers, developers, and administrators.

In the year 2001, she faced a crisis. The CFO said he could no longer allocate the large amount she had previously received and he cut her budget by more than 50 percent. Faced with no alternative, she had to lay off staff, reduce programs, and eliminate a number of programs. Managers and employees were upset by the lack of development programs. Some had been part way through a curriculum and found it suddenly gone.

This is a frequent occurrence for corporate universities who have relied on a single source of funding and have not built a business case for what they contribute. Business units would most likely have gladly paid for needed training, but because of the easy allocation process, this corporate university director had never thought of implementing a chargeback model.

A multinational organization has a corporate university with a mix of funding models. Organized along the federal model, the corporate headquarters of the corporate university receives 80 percent of its funding from an allocation. This is basically derived from a "tax" that all operating units pay to cover the costs of leadership development, knowledge capture and dissemination, and a common information system to tackle development activities.

Each business unit has a division of the corporate university. These are required to recover up to 80 percent of their costs through charging back the costs of their services to the individual departments and managers within the unit. Their only allocation is for space and utilities.

This funding model puts responsibility and financial accountability as low in the organization as possible and gives managers control over development costs. However, the corporate support allows for solid leadership development and visibility as to who is being developed.

The area where almost all corporate universities struggle is that of securing a reliable and long-term source of funding. In a handful of organizations, the corporate university enjoys CEO-level support and funding. However, for most, the challenge is to demonstrate value to their customers of a sufficient level to ensure ongoing funding. This chapter focuses on three primary funding models that corporate universities have developed.

The Three Funding Models

There are three basic approaches to funding a corporate university, and in this chapter, we will explore the pros and cons in relation to your strategy, scope, and corporate expectations.

Corporate Allocation Model

This is the most common and oldest of the three models. In this model, all expenses incurred by the corporate university are considered part of the general operating overhead for the firm, and all costs are allocated to the profit centers according to some internal process. Often, budgets are established once a year, generally with minimal thought to planning what training or development needs may exist. Frequently, the past year's budget is used as a base with some percentage added on for growth, inflation, or whatever. The staff of the corporate university is expected to stay within that budget. Headcounts and many other expenses are considered fixed, making it very difficult to add more staff or to reduce staff when needs change.

Partial or Full Cost Recovery Model

Under this model, the corporate university charges individuals and departments for the costs they actually incur for training. This means that the corporate university operates more or less as a business, itself. It needs to recover an amount equal to or greater than whatever it cost to develop and deliver the training. This has become popular in larger companies over the past decade. The university or training department is expected to internally "sell" programs to employees for a fee that will at least partially recover the costs associated with the program. A small portion of the total costs may be allocated to profit centers, but some percentage of the total should be recovered through *chargebacks*—internal charges to the people who actually take the classes or use the services.

Profit Center Model

Under this model, classes and programs are "sold" to customers internally and, sometimes, externally, for a profit. The training function or corporate university does not "cost" the company anything and may actually bring money in. Motorola University, as well as parts of the training functions at General Electric and Xerox, have adopted this approach. Most classes are open to anyone, including other companies or the public. Costs are competitive with other vendors.

Choice of a Funding Model

In many organizations you will not have much say over which model is chosen. Many corporate universities are launched with the expectation that they will recover costs or that they will receive all funding from corporate allocations. However, whichever model you choose or have chosen for you will have a lot to say about the kinds of programs you can offer and how effective the corporate university will be.

Make funding a topic for the consideration of your governance committee. You should go over the different models, including any special ones your organization may have, and discuss the pros and cons of each. The committee members must be aware of the consequences and limitations for each model, so they have expectations aligned with what you can resource and fund.

Before reading further, complete Exercise 7.1 on page 80. Use your answers to the exercise in combination with Template 7.1 to help determine which model may work best for your corporate university. Then compare your answers to the following section, which gives you some guidelines on the pros and cons of each model.

EXERCISE 7.1

Pros and Cons

Before reviewing the models in detail to decide which is most appropriate for your corporate university, please start by thinking of one to two pros and cons for each and write them in the spaces provided.

Corporate Allocation Model

Pros:

_____

_____

_____

Cons:

_____

_____

_____

Partial or Full Cost Recovery Model

Pros:

_____

_____

_____

Cons:

_____

_____

_____

Profit Center Model

Pros:

_____

_____

_____

Cons:

_____

_____

_____

Alternative Funding Models

Corporate Allocation Model

Pros:

Cons:

Cost Recovery Model

Pros:

Cons:

Profit Center Model

Pros:

Cons:

Designed by Eileen Clegg

Corporate Allocation

Pros

- Provides a stable and known base from which to operate.

- The corporate university staff does not have to "sell" programs, but can respond to the development needs within the firm.

- Allows for continuity of programs.

Cons

- Offers almost no flexibility. If a sudden need occurs, something else will have to be cut or the staff will have to ask for a special budget override or increase.

- Increasingly, line managers are resentful of being taxed for programs that do not directly benefit them.

- Doesn't require staff to rethink or reexamine programs to see whether they are really needed or are producing results.

- Discourages innovation and new programs, as they will have to be defended and "fought for" in the annual budgeting process.

- Does not provide any incentive for staff to work closely with line management to meet their specific needs.

Partial or Total Cost Recovery

Pros

- Gives managers some control over their expenditures, and allows them to pay primarily for what their employees use.

- Focuses the corporate university staff on providing courses and development activities that meet actual needs of line managers.

- By having some of the costs allocated, allows many routine programs to be sustained.

- Provides for some flexibility in staffing levels by allowing increased staff whenever program fees cover the cost.

- Builds-in flexibility—any class or program can be developed and offered at any time a manager (or several managers) are willing to pay for it.

Cons

- Requires the corporate university staff to "sell" services and programs and to market their abilities to the firm. Some may see this as a negative, although others find it a strength.

- Takes away some of the stability provided by the allocation model.

- Becomes difficult to administer and track who is getting which development opportunity—this method requires that a training tracking system exist within the company.

- Requires time to market, sell, and provide benefit for a range of people, often requiring the corporate university staff to develop coalitions of managers to pay for a program. There is always a risk that a group will either back out of their agreement before the program is completed or that they will not pay. This can cause significant internal accounting problems.

Profit Center Model

Pros

- Looks extremely attractive to any executive who is concerned with developing the workforce and making money.

- Almost guarantees that classes will meet needs of the students. If they didn't, the students wouldn't have signed up and paid for them.

- Allows the corporate university staff great flexibility in offering courses that can gather enough interest to pay for themselves and return a profit.

Cons

- Encourages popularity over need or utility.

- Does not provide a mechanism for the corporation to mandate development (for example, leadership or management training).

- Can be exploited. A corporate university leader can curry favor with a general manager and focus too much attention on a single unit.

- No incentive to control costs.

Implications of Funding Models

Funding models, like all other parts of the corporate university, need to be aligned with the strategic approach you have chosen. Below are some thoughts on each model and which funding model makes the most sense.

Change Management Focus

Because change is never popular, this strategic approach is hard to fund with the profit center model. Across all the corporate universities we have studied, those that are change focused have relied on central funding. Usually change initiatives are the outcome of the CEO and the senior leadership team agreeing that some dramatic and rapid differences need to occur. They then allocate the resources to make that happen. The most difficult aspect of this is to use the funds wisely for maximum impact.

Although you may not have to account for how the funds are spent on a monthly or even quarterly basis, you will eventually have to show that the programs you delivered made a difference. If they did not, your funding will disappear. Once the change programs are established and are having an impact, some organizations move to a partial cost recovery model. In this case, the business units are asked to pay on a per-person basis for the development or training that takes place. It is also common for the business units to pay all the travel and other expenses incurred by an employee while attending one of these programs.

Strategic or Business Focus

Business initiatives are almost always funded at the corporate or divisional level. When a program such as Six Sigma Quality or when a leadership development program gets started, the corporation usually allocates funding—at least in the beginning. Many of these programs start at the top, with senior management getting some education in the initiative. They are then asked to fund the ongoing rollout in their own divisions with their own funds.

So once again, there are transition models whereby the corporate university can quickly move from allocation to cost recovery and perhaps, over time, to the profit center model. This is what happened at Motorola with the quality programs. At first, they were funded by corporate. Over time, the business units picked up the costs on a per-employee basis, and today the programs are available to any of us for a fee, and they return a profit to Motorola.

Skill and Development Focus

This is the type of strategic focus where you have funding choices. The most common model for corporate universities using this approach is the corporate allocation model. However, this model contains many negatives, as we discussed above. The biggest among them is the lack of accountability on the part of the business unit and employee. Employees can sign up for a wide range of classes, as long as they meet certain prerequisites. This can lead to people attending classes they do not need and that have little business value. Managers use these classes as an employee perk—a way to make an employee feel better or to build morale—rather than as a way to improve actual competence or build skills.

A better model is the cost recovery one, where each employee is charged through his or her manager for the class. This way, business units and managers are directly accountable for training. Some organizations provide employees with a personal development budget that they use as they wish to attend seminars, classes, conferences, or other development activities.

External Customer Focus

The funding for this approach is normally the profit center model, although often the classes are prepaid in the cost of the equipment the customer bought. Sometimes your organization might offer development opportunities to customers or potential customers as a means of increasing the sales of other products or services. In this case, the costs may be covered by corporate allocations.

Action Steps

Work with your governance committee and discuss the different models and their implications. Match your choice to your strategic orientation and to the culture of your organization. If you have no choice in the model, and you feel it is the wrong one, use your governance committee to try and have it changed. Perhaps work out an evolutionary approach that will slowly move you toward the model you feel is best.

Remember, these are ideal models and most organizations have models that are combinations of these. Some programs may be paid for by allocation whereas other programs are delivered only when people are willing to pay for them. Most large corporate universities end up with combinations of these, but they still need to be chosen based on well-thought-out criteria.

Conclusion

Having chosen a particular funding model does not mean that you will use that model indefinitely. It is a way to create a foundation of fiscal responsibility and accountability that can be tweaked as your corporate university changes. It is also a model that may be handed down to you from the CFO or from other executives, and it may not be possible to make your own choice of model.

Remember as well that it is possible to combine funding models, and that the optimum solution may not become clear until your corporate university is fully under way. For now though, it is important to move forward with the model you have chosen so that as you bring the different departments and employees on board, everyone knows the beginning ground rules. This will free you to begin looking at the central aspect of the corporate university— the design and delivery of your curriculum, the subject of Chapter Eight.

Chapter 8

Performance Analysis and Development Delivery

IT IS BETTER to be successful at architecting and delivering a few powerful learning experiences than to have a whole catalog of unfulfilled expectations.

Company X has a fat catalogue of classes that are disconnected from any business result or goal. This is the type of learning that is increasingly ineffective in helping organizations achieve business objectives. Company X has a large training and development function that offers more than two hundred classes annually, with more than half delivered in the classroom through external and internal instructors. Although these classes are often requested by individuals, and in fact are not usually delivered until a minimum number of employees have signed up, they rarely meet any clear business need. Moreover, if an employee did want one of these classes for a legitimate business purpose, he or she might have to wait weeks or months to take the class. Much of the training is delivered simply to meet arbitrary "learning" targets established by management, again with no direct bearing on business results. Although Company X may be successful at the current time, the training and development activities are unlikely to be supported during recessionary times, nor are they likely to be credited for any of the organization's success in the marketplace.

Micropower University in Sao Paulo, Brazil, has an integrated approach to curriculum with a "learning portal." Content is updated daily and reviewed weekly at a meeting attended by managers, executives, and marketing people who identify business needs. The learning portal provides virtual classes on what employees need to know for day-to-day work. "We are very focused on results," said Francisco Antonio Soeltl, president of Micropower. In each business unit, there are mentors for different skills and competencies as needed. Employees may have one, two, or three mentors in different subject areas. There is a blend of action learning, coaching, e-learning, and classroom "day-to-day activities." Evaluation of learning takes place on the job by team members who are facilitators and evaluators. "We can see if people get knowledge from the training," said Soeltl. "Learning is not a benefit; it is part of the job. It is our responsibility to learn."

This chapter discusses what a curriculum is in the context of a corporate university and explores various ways you can foster and deliver learning. It includes a discussion of how organizational learning is moving from the notion of training for individual success alone to development to help individuals achieve business goals. It talks about how to place an emphasis on performance improvement and how to use both formal and informal learning to do this, and how important it is that both content and delivery be tied to the strategic direction you have chosen and to the culture of your organization.

Strategic Value

Especially in the beginning, the corporate university cannot be all things to all people. Directly affecting its reputation and effectiveness will be the perception among the governance committee and stakeholders of the corporate university's ability to produce the expected results. Corporate education should focus on closing gaps that have been uncovered between what the company wants to be able to do and what it can really do because of the employees' lack of knowledge or skills. Effective learning should take the least amount of time away from producing the product or delivering the service, and should be immediately useful.

This means the corporate university educators have to be up-to-date on the business and the issues it faces from competition, from change, and from improvements or additions to knowledge in the field. Then these same people have to be able to anticipate the gaps and offer programs and learning events, and structure activities that will close the gaps—preferably before they are ever issues. Few corporate universities have successfully closed the gaps for a number of reasons. First, most are focused on training as an event, not a process. They are concerned with delivery, not content. They focus on the immediate, not the long term. Table 8.1 lists the traditional ideas around development and training and points out how these are changing.

TABLE 8.1

The Transition of Training

From Training for Training's Sake	To Training for Business Success
Characterized by	Characterized by
No particular client	Clear link to business needs
No clear business need	Alignment to corporate strategic direction
No assessment of performance deficiency or need	Assessment of performance deficiency or need
No effort to embed learning in the work process	Close partnership with business to embed learning in work process
No measurement of effectiveness	Measurement of effectiveness

Performance Analysis

Leading-edge firms are moving away from simply responding to a learning request by offering a class. Instead they are using a much more business-focused consulting process that will help identify performance gaps that are caused by lack of skills or competencies. In this process, the trainer (usually at this point called a performance consultant) works with management to determine what business goals need to be accomplished and where the current gaps in skills, knowledge, or understanding lie. In collaboration, they lay out a strategy to close these gaps. Some of the solutions may require training. Other solutions may require a learning event or some other similar activity, and still others may require the people involved to actually have experience doing something.

For example, if a company decides to begin doing business in China, it might identify knowledge of Chinese business practices as a knowledge gap. The corporate university might work with management to develop strategies to close the gap. Appropriate activities might include training about Chinese business practices, business structures, and the Chinese government, and even perhaps language training. Other activities might include a trip to China to meet officials and experience the issues and environment first-hand. Management might assemble a project team to take on the first phase of expansion, and perhaps debrief periodically with a mentor, professor, or China expert. In this systematic way, the company takes advantages of a variety of tools and methods to achieve its business goals smoothly.

Methodologies

A curriculum is an interconnected series of learning experiences all focused around a single theme or topic that is dictated by the learning outcome that is needed. A curriculum may consist of formal classes, but outstanding curriculums also include a variety of activities, both formal and informal, that lead to learning.

A good curriculum is holistic. It is not necessarily a classroom experience. It's an orchestra of events and experiences that inspire individuals to do something substantially different from what they did before. Good curricula meet real business needs that training staff and line management have collaboratively identified.

A variety of methods and tools are used to ensure that the concepts and skills are learned and reinforced. These include web-based training, classroom discussion, group projects and activities, coaching, reading, hands-on experience, experiential learning activities, action learning, and more. Employees also need to receive continuous feedback and should periodically review and re-assess the competencies that they are acquiring.

Classes, by themselves and unconnected to business needs, are mostly a waste of time and money for all parties involved. The popularity of a course is not necessarily a sign of effectiveness. The design of any learning activity should take into account the learner's background, work environment, learning content, and opportunities for reinforcement.

There is a tendency in corporate education to focus on formal (or classroom) learning, yet recent research shows that informal learning is a far more typical way for people to learn. The U.S. Department of Labor Statistics (http://www.bls.gov/news.release/sept.t02.htm) estimates that 70 percent or more of learning occurs outside formal training activities. As Charles Handy says, "The best learning happens in real life with real problems and real people and not in classrooms" (1989, pp. 56-57). New employees learn from each other and from making many small errors, which are quickly corrected by a coworker or a supervisor. Employees learn by watching and listening to others around them and by scanning documents and the Internet.

As Figure 8.1 shows, the greatest learning impact, in this case the most retention and utilization of what was learned, occurs with informal learning.

Next, complete Exercise 8.1 on page 90 to help you think about various delivery methods.

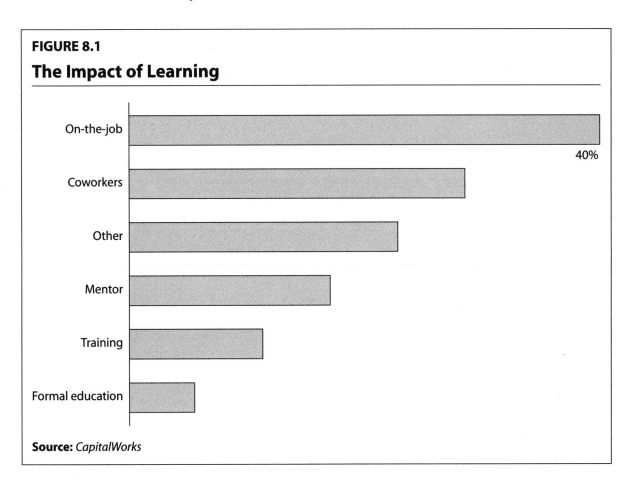

FIGURE 8.1

The Impact of Learning

Source: *CapitalWorks*

EXERCISE 8.1

Delivery Methods

Think about a series of classes you offer on a single topic (for example, leadership development). Take a few moments and indicate what percentage of that training is delivered by each of the following methods (the total should equal 100 percent):

_____ Stand-up lecture/traditional classroom

_____ Small discussion groups/tutorials

_____ Self-study books/worksheets

_____ Electronic Performance Support Systems (EPSS)

_____ Videotapes with or without workbook

_____ Satellite programs/distance learning

_____ e-Learning or Internet-based learning

_____ Action learning teams/project-based teams

_____ Simulations (computer or face-to-face)

_____ Storytelling

_____ Coaching or mentoring

An ideal learning experience will consist of some mix of these. For example, one organization requires all aspiring managers to complete an online e-learning program. This program consists of a rigorous set of courses designed to ensure that the student has mastered all the basics. There are tests and opportunities for the student to restudy areas of weakness. The goal is for the student to master a body of legal and policy fundamentals around supervision and management. It is designed to be taken whenever convenient for the employee and is specific to the organization.

When an employee has completed the e-learning courses successfully, he or she can then move on to a series of classes where case studies of actual situations are discussed and some hands-on practice in managing a team can take place with a mentor. This mentor is an experienced manager who has agreed to let the student shadow her or him and see how a manager really gets work done.

After meeting the standards that were established for performance and knowledge, the student is promoted to manager and given a management position. There is a one-year ongoing program of seminars and discussion groups to continue the education process. The corporate university has also developed an online chat room where the new manager can air problems and get expert advice.

To further reinforce what was learned, they also developed a website with three sections. The first section is a Resource Center, which contains a virtual library of books, articles, and videos on management topics, as well as a number of searchable cases on common management topics and issues. The second section consists of a manager's forum, which is a bulletin board where questions on difficult issues can be posted. Managers who have previously graduated from the program post responses and suggest solutions. The third section provides an e-mail and chat room function for senior management to communicate with the students on critical topics.

We have provided Template 8.1 to help you specifically think about ways to include informal learning in the corporate university. Increasingly, educators are recognizing that informal learning is powerful and may be more important than formal learning in helping learners actually apply and customize the learning to their own needs.

Selection of Delivery Methods

Whether one chooses to use multimedia, the Internet, or the classroom to deliver training depends on the level of content versus the level of understanding required to master the material. The delivery method selected should be decided based on a number of factors. These include the skill level of course developers, the availability of equipment and resources, the type of material to be taught, the skill level and attitude of trainees, the time available, and the organization's familiarity with the chosen method.

Entry-level concepts, simple facts, basic procedures, and anything that can be shown or simulated effectively can all be delivered in an automated format, such as through web-based or computer-based training. Examples of courses or material that can be delivered in this way include safety training, how to install or use a piece of equipment, and problems such as those found in mathematics, physics, or chemistry.

Supervisory training that focuses on learning legal requirements or illustrating procedures such as hiring, interviewing, and disciplining an employee can also be effectively delivered in an e-learning format.

More complex or conceptual material is still best mastered in a group setting or with the close help of a mentor or teacher. Examples include discussions about ethics, leadership development, career coaching and counseling, and similar materials. A mix of media, such as that described in Exercise 8.1, is becoming the preferred method of delivery.

Conclusion

Having closely examined the different delivery models for your courses, you will be in a position to work with your staff, and to a lesser degree your governance committee, to match content with the optimum methods of delivery. As you begin to articulate not only the *what* but also the *how* and *why* of your courses, you will flesh out a picture of what your corporate university has to offer. However, having a great corporate university isn't enough—people need to know about it. In the next chapter, we will look at how to communicate your offerings to people throughout your organization.

Curriculm Brainstorm Process

Curriculum Brainstorm Process

Consider the Opportunities for Informal Learning for a Well-Rounded Curriculum

Do We Have In-House Expertise?

Could One Take a Trip to Have an Immersion Experience?

Communities of Practice Already Under Way on the Subject:

Desired Learning Outcome:

e-Learning:

FaF Classes

Are There Great Books on the Subject?

People Who Might Be Interviewed or Serve as Advisors:

Designed by Eileen Clegg

Chapter 9

Marketing to Build Brand, Relationships, and Success

IF YOU EFFECTIVELY COMMUNICATE the strategic intent and benefits of your corporate university throughout the organization, you will gain the credibility, input, and support necessary for sustainability. This makes for the easiest kind of marketing—disseminating information about something you believe in.

We know of three multinational corporations whose initially successful corporate universities gained great outside recognition and kudos, only to slowly lose their internal credibility and influence. You would probably recognize the names because they have all been the subjects of laudatory articles, books, or media coverage. In all three cases, they communicated and leveraged their initial early internal successes to the outside world. Unfortunately, they were marketed as great ideas to the outside world, but little was done to market them internally. They did have good ideas, which impressed and inspired other organizations. But they did not have the metrics, management support, and internal relationships that create strong bonds between the corporate university and the rest of the organization. Today one of these corporate universities is gone entirely, another has been entirely revamped, and the third is a small shadow of its initial presence in the organization.

IBM has built a management leadership development program that is highly focused, well designed and delivered, and has proven to be very effective at developing leadership for IBM. This program also has extremely deep credibility internally. Most people outside the organization know little of this: IBM spends virtually no time communicating externally. Instead, there is an ongoing, multilayered approach to marketing this program internally. Management travels around the world to meet with business units to describe the leadership programs. The programs are required for promotion and advancement. They have metrics demonstrating value. IBM believes in the leadership program and makes sure that people throughout the organization know why.

If the corporate university is perceived as an isolated function, disconnected from the business and serving narrow interests, it will fail. How management and employees see the corporate university and its contribution to business success is not only important, it may make the difference as to whether you get resources, staff, or management interest and support. This chapter focuses on how you can shape the way employees see you by the messages you communicate. It lays out some methods that you can use to ensure that your success is well known and that critical information gets to the people who make decisions about funding and other resources. The chapter helps you craft messages that let everyone know what you do and how you add value.

Your Marketing Challenge

By this point in the workbook, whether you realize it or not, you have developed several foundational elements for a marketing strategy. Through the first eight chapters, you have answered the following questions: Why create a corporate university? What objectives are planned? Who will it serve? What will it serve? By whom will it be served? What values will it provide the customer and the organization? How will it be funded? (Don't forget to fund the marketing effort of your corporate university too.)

It's time now to put on your marketer's cap and (1) gather the answers to these questions from earlier exercises and (2) write down what you think to be the strengths, weaknesses, opportunities, and threats (SWOT) of your corporate university. These will be the foundation for communicating what it is you are building. Although it is not the purpose of this workbook to provide a Marketing 101 primer, it is critical to understand why marketing your corporate university is vital to its short- and long-term success.

Building successful relationships throughout the organization will depend on your ability to realistically communicate your goals and accomplishments internally, and accurately measure your success in a way that is acceptable to the organization. You will need a well-defined strategy, the right message, and a robust system for disseminating and measuring success. In other words—a marketing plan.

Remember, marketing is not simply the glamour of advertising and communications—the glory of the brand—it involves a sound, well-defined marketing structure and operating plan. You must start by being able to answer all of the following questions:

- What, why, and who is your corporate university? Who are your customers and your competition?

- What is your elevator speech? (See Exercise 9.1 on page 96 for assistance on this.)

- What will your corporate university be named, and what will its brand be? Remember not to confuse *brand* with *logo*. Your logo is just part of the brand. Your brand is what your customers will think and say about you the very last time they interact with the corporate university. What do you want them to think and say? That is your brand goal, and it is a constantly moving and evolving target.

- What are the strengths, weaknesses, opportunities, and threats (SWOT) presented to and by the corporate university? Write these down (use that worksheet you borrowed from your marketing friend).

- What are your goals for success? How will your success be defined by the corporate university's staff, its governance committee, its customers, and by senior management of the organization?

- How will you measure that success? What will be important to know from your customers before, during, and after an interaction with the corporate university? Were your customers satisfied? Did you meet your customer's expectations? Did you know their expectations before they walked in or signed in online? How will you gather, analyze, and disseminate this information?

- Which are the most effective methods for communicating new services internally to your customers, or externally if you are an external customer focused model?

- What messages will produce the greatest impact on changing behavior among your target groups? There will be several to develop. Remember, your marketing is not geared only toward your target customers but also toward the corporate university's staff, governance committee, and senior management.

With this information in hand, your challenge is to construct a plan for systematically introducing the corporate university to all its potential stakeholders, users, and supporters. This means that you will need separate efforts for executives, line and functional managers, and employees in general. Your efforts should be carefully planned and carried out over time, and it should begin before you are ready to "open your doors" to your customers.

EXERCISE 9.1

The Elevator Speech

In the space below, write twenty-five to fifty words explaining how your corporate university is different from a training and development function and how it adds value to your organization. This will be your elevator speech—your verbal advertisement that quickly and clearly explains the what and why of the corporate university should you, hypothetically, be asked, So what is this corporate university all about? while traveling in an elevator with a stakeholder, employee, or the CEO.

Marketing Partners

People chartered with launching a corporate university can come from a variety of backgrounds and do not necessarily have marketing or communications expertise. And if you do not have this expertise, you may feel a bit overwhelmed with the marketing questions and challenges just presented to you. Do your best on your own, but by all means, build relationships with professionals who do have this expertise—and engage them. Your partners in marketing the corporate university should include representatives from whatever internal departments your organization has that focus on communications or marketing. Many large companies have dedicated staff for communicating with employees, as well as a marketing department that is focused on the external market and on customers. You should work out arrangements with them to create an ongoing series of marketing messages. Think of your organization as your client and market to it just as you would market your company's products to consumers.

Enlist staff support in helping identify the responses to the marketing questions defined earlier. Don't wait to get started on this. It will take time—weeks, maybe months—to clearly define your marketing plan and supporting structure and to create your communication vehicles. The marketing plan should be developed on the footsteps of finalizing the decisions and plans as defined by this workbook's earlier chapters. It's an evolutionary process and we recommend you get started now. Use Template 9.1 to collect answers to questions in this chapter. Assuming that you will answer each of the questions above, we'll focus now on finding the best messages.

What's the Message?

All too often people think it is self-evident that training is valuable—but statistics show that this is the first area often hit by budget cuts. With the development of a corporate university, you have an opportunity to reframe messages about the value of training and learning. By using stories about how the corporate university improved performance or helped reduce errors, you will build credibility. It takes an aggressive communications approach to get above the usual flood of information employees are exposed to. You need to find as many ways as possible to explain what you are doing, why you are doing it, and what the results have been.

You must begin, however, with identifying the messages that most resonate and affect behavioral change among your customers and stakeholders. Once you have brainstormed your messages, test them out by asking selected executives, managers, and employees for their reaction to them.

Crafting Your Marketing Plan

Road Map:

Communication Tools:

Elevator Pitch:

Key Messages:

Ideas:

Using surveys, focus groups, or informal interviews will help you identify what those messages may be. These research tools can be used to discover what your customer's needs are and get feedback on some of your proposed messages.

Ask whether the messages seem frank and honest and whether they are clear and are believable. Many internal organizational public relations and communication efforts are immediately identified as "corporate speak" and are discounted or not accepted by the employees. Obviously, you need to try not to let this happen. One tactic is to allow the employees to write the basic message themselves. Form a brainstorming group and ask its members to come up with several key messages that can be included in the communications that you use.

The value of research here cannot be overstated. Some advanced data collection can save you from building the wrong brand, delivering the wrong message, and possibly losing the credibility of the corporate university overall—all of which could take months or years to overcome.

Here are some insights into what your customers may be thinking—or not thinking—about your corporate university. Employees are frequently confused about why the corporate university is different from the training department. They may think that the training department has simply changed its name, and unfortunately they are often correct. While you are deep into the work of creating the corporate university, sometimes it's hard to remember that outsiders may not have a clue as to what you are doing or why. It is best to assume that others know little or nothing about your corporate university's existence and purpose to the organization. It will be up to you to change that. Two critical explanations must be made clear to all employees: (1) what the difference is between a corporate university and a training function and (2) how the corporate university adds value.

Different Strategies, Different Messages

Your marketing messages should reflect the strategic function of your corporate university and should reinforce the strategic direction you have decided to undertake.

Change Management Focused

If you are trying to drive change through the organization, your message will be about the value of the change, and how change occurs at both a macro level and the level of individual performance. You will explain how the corporate university serves to integrate the skills, attitudes, and cultural shifts necessary to affect organizationwide change and then reinforces that change by providing any new skills or competencies that are developed.

The career development aspects of the corporate university can also be explained and showcased.

Change management marketing messages might point out how the corporate university helped individuals gain the skills they needed to be effective in the changed organization, or how the corporate university prepared employees before the changes occurred so they lost less time adjusting to the changes and were able to remain employed. Other messages might focus on how your efforts lessened employee anxiety and reduced turnover of valuable people.

Skill and Development Focused

If your corporation is designed around improving competencies and building skills, your message will emphasize that a corporate university is the most effective way to bring people up to speed by using a variety of delivery types, including e-learning. Employees who have the skills they need to do the job are probably going to do it faster and with higher quality, less frustration, and more satisfaction than are people who learn by trial and error or who are never sure whether they are doing the job properly.

Specific messages can showcase successful employees who are testimonials for the corporate university's ability to quickly impart new skills or to get new employees up to speed quickly. The faster employees become productive, the less they cost the organization and the faster they can help raise revenues. Messages should not only focus on activities but also on the outcomes that were achieved.

Business Development Focused

When business development is the focus of the corporate university, it is critical to convey the difference between old style training and a business focused corporate university. Rather than simply transferring skill sets, you are preparing people for success at or to create new businesses. Show and stress the ongoing integrated approaches to learning that should characterize any corporate university effort.

To function at this level in the organization, employees need to have expert knowledge and be able to communicate and influence others. The corporate university should highlight the activities it undertook to help employees gain this expert knowledge and learn how to communicate and influence. Examples, stories, and even testimonials are appropriate.

External Customer Focused

When promoting the corporate university to the external customer, it is vital to explain how the corporate university will use the latest technologies to help the customer acquire needed skills as quickly and inexpensively as possible. Internally, you need to make sure employees know that the effort you are making is to increase customer satisfaction and expand the customer's ability to use your product or service so that they will purchase more.

Cisco Systems offers training to network administrators, as does Microsoft, and both have leveraged these classes to build market share. When a person has a certificate from one of these organizations, he or she is very motivated to influence their employers to buy more of the equipment or software. The graduates also become referral marketing advocates and recommend the classes to others. Both companies have probably increased sales because of the marketing impact of their students.

If this is your strategic direction, the marketing themes should stress how much more efficient the graduates have become and how much the quality of their work has changed. Messages can also focus on the graduates' reaction to the training. You can use testimonials from graduates and even showcase how they are using the skills back on the job, or how they have improved their own professional marketability with a certification from a reputable corporate university.

Action Steps: Before the Launch

Prior to actually opening the doors, you should have already spread the word about the corporate university. Once your governance committee and structure are in place and your strategy and scope are clear, you are ready to begin constructing a marketing and communications plan. Some of the key points to communicate to stakeholders at this stage include

1. Why you are starting this corporate university.

2. Who will benefit from it?

3. Who has sponsored its creation? Why?

4. What are the corporate expectations from the university?

Go back and look at your elevator speech, use Template 9.1 and Exercise 9.1, engage with your internal partners, and improve the pitch to the point that everyone remembers and starts using it. Though you will be using a variety of media and messages, each message needs to underline the benefits to the customer from the corporate university, and each must explain why the university was created and what outcomes it will produce for the organization.

Next, complete Exercise 9.2 on page 102 to help you develop different messages for your various audiences.

EXERCISE 9.2

Different Messages for Different Audiences

Write down the two to three key messages you feel should be sent to the employees of your organization. Put an EX in front of the most significant message for the executive team, an M for the message most appropriate for the managers, and an E in front of the one most important for the employees in general.

Message #1: _____

_____

_____

_____

_____

_____

_____

_____

Message #2: _____

_____

_____

_____

_____

_____

_____

_____

Message #3: _____

_____

_____

_____

_____

_____

_____

_____

Communication Tools

As you work with your internal marketing and communications experts, you may want to consider some of the following techniques for communicating:

- Take some of the templates you have developed during the process of using this book—for example, the strategy templates (Templates 2.1 and 2.2) or the structure template (Template 5.1)—and have your marketing department's graphic artists polish them into visuals to post on your organization's intranet.

- Ask your marketing department partners for advice on the history of effective internal communications—and strongly consider using the same vehicles and marketing channels.

- Ask some of your target customers how they'd prefer to learn about the corporate university, and use the marketing channels most frequently suggested.

- Use the filled-out templates to enhance PowerPoint presentations.

- Send e-mails with postings about the development of the corporate university (use this medium judiciously for maximum effect).

- Develop a website to promote the corporate university—or if you're delivering e-learning as part of your model, be sure to add some marketing flair to the site design. Cross-market the corporate university's section of your internal or external facing website(s) by linking from other sections of the site, or build banner or text-based "ads" and place them on other popular sections of the sites to build awareness and drive traffic.

- Include your messages in organizational newsletters or e-zines.

- Ask your CEO or human resources executive to write a letter to the employees about their own vision for the corporate university.

- Create posters for bulletin boards, banners to hang from rafters, or large signs to place on easels in lobbies, cafeterias, or other common traffic zones.

- Partner with payroll to include a flyer or postcard with employee paychecks.

- Create some promotional items ("tchotchkes"), such as t-shirts, stress-relief balls, and pens, or have a programmer create a corporate university screensaver for disseminating to each employee's computer.

- Develop your own video presentations (use available production resources to help you).

- Have managers talk about the corporate university from scripts you prepare and make available to them.

- Be sure recruiters are "talking up" the new corporate university to applicants, and ensure you have some marketing information available to new hires through your on-boarding or assimilation processes.

- Provide materials in all the languages your organization uses. And be sure your messages are global if you are a global firm.

Marketing Events

In addition to sending messages, you may consider planning activities that will help carry your message and rally support for the corporate university. Many event possibilities exist; here are a few ideas:

- Hold a corporate university fair during lunchtime. Set up booths staffed by corporate university advocates, who tell employees the purpose and scope of the university. Offer raffle prizes and desserts to encourage employees to come. It is always best to prepare some information (posters, flyers, or short videos) ahead of time. However, we have found it most valuable to be there in person to listen to concerns, field questions, and make suggestions.

- Feature the corporate university as a segment during an employee communication meeting. Senior management can talk about why they stand behind the corporate university and the results they expect to see. Someone from the corporate university can talk about the specific range of learning opportunities and how employees can get involved. Get input from employees and make it clear you are interested in their ideas and will use them.

- Prepare a presentation about the corporate university that can be taken to staff meetings. Include plenty of time for questions and answers.

This prelaunch communication is essential to success. People feel that they have been a part of the creation and that the corporate university is an organic function, rising out of needs that the organization has, and that it will be useful. Corporate universities that arise in a vacuum are rarely accepted and rarely achieve the level of success that would be possible if they included the thinking and emotions of those who will be using them. Finally, remember, according to the laws of advertising, behavioral change takes time. You must begin preselling what you are building and what you will deliver to build critical mass among your customers and stakeholders so that they will be "on your doorstep" the day you open for business.

Action Steps: Marketing After the Launch

Once the doors are opened, expectations are always very high. All your prelaunch communication has created the idea that major things will happen right away. So you should have a few activities or programs planned that will highlight the things the university will do. Here is a list of some tips for maximizing your messages immediately after the launch:

- As with any business, the most credible advertising is by word-of-mouth from satisfied customers. Big wins on very targeted learning opportunities will yield the best results.

- Offer a short seminar on some currently "hot" topic. Bring in an outside speaker and make sure the seminar is fast-paced, business-focused, and stimulates the attendees. Invite a selected number of key employees to attend—those who will communicate what happened back to their friends and associates.

- Have at least one to two classes available right from day one for each segment of the employee population. Do not launch until you have these programs or courses ready. To open without them is analogous to opening a department store and having no merchandise to sell. Employees, especially upper management, need to see that their money is being used for something they can see and are familiar with.

- Use the corporate university as a place for managers to hold staff or communication meetings. By doing this, employees will become familiar with the location and see your offerings, which you should have carefully posted. You can also supply literature about the university.

- Find ways to communicate your success regularly. A consistent method of communicating what the corporate university has accomplished will build credibility with senior management. This does *not* mean communicating how many have attended classes or how many classes have been held. Rather, your focus should be on accomplishments, changes, and the impact that the corporate university is having on the organization.

One of the hardest parts about marketing a new corporate university is explaining what you do *not* do. It is important to set boundaries so that you do not become trapped offering too many things that do not fully satisfy anyone. Your corporate communication group can be a wonderful resource to you. Work with them to develop a communication plan.

Conclusion

Every organization has different audiences and different offerings. Unfortunately, those who are closest to the match between audience and offering often are the least able to explain and "advertise" the value. In order to develop an objective and clear statement of your corporate university, it is wise to work with a group to create a clear picture that can easily be shared with others. We encourage you to use the templates and exercises in this chapter to begin "tooting your own horn" and to partner with a group of marketing people who can contribute language and spirit to carry forward your marketing plan.

Chapter 10

Metrics for Measuring Success

ULTIMATELY THE ONLY DETERMINATION of the corporate university's success is if it can demonstrate, in a measurable way, that it has had an effect on the successful execution of the organization's strategy.

Facing the CEO is often a bit nerve-racking, but it's even more so when you are not sure what you will be asked. A corporate university executive was faced with that situation and paid a price for not having spent the time to really understand what this most important stakeholder expected. After the corporate university executive had made a presentation filled with numbers showing all the activity that the corporate university had been engaged in over the past quarter, the CEO said, "I see that most of our management team has completed the performance management curriculum. That's fine. But has there been any improvement in employee attitudes toward management or in our turnover?" A simple, but disquieting, question because the corporate university leader had no data at all about either. When he could not answer, the CEO said, "Just what I expected," and left the room.

Measures can be both qualitative and quantitative. We tend to place most of our faith and trust in quantifiable ones, but it is often the qualitative measures that make a difference. In the early 1990s, National Semiconductor was in transition. It had hired a new CEO after the retirement of its founder, was reengineering its products, and was challenged with market competition and a recession. The corporate university was launched in this environment with a charter to drive change. The change process the university developed included a variety of activities consisting of off-sites, seminars, classes, and team-building and other collaboration events. Slowly word got out that the activities were useful and that they were relevant and engaging. Employees lined up to get into the programs, and even reluctant managers began to say positive things about the university. The unspoken metrics that were later translated into more quantifiable ones were relevance, usefulness, and practicality. If these had not been part of the program, it would not have been as successful, nor would it have convinced skeptical managers. Numbers would not have convinced them either. This was one of those times when actions spoke much louder than numbers would have.

Measuring and showing the success of a corporate university is perhaps the most difficult thing to do. Almost everyone struggles with this, yet it can be a straightforward process. If you have followed the processes we have described in this book and have a clear strategy and set of goals, measuring your accomplishments toward achieving those goals should not be hard. The biggest problem people have with measuring value is determining what value is up front with the stakeholders. If you take the time to do this in your governance committee and with other stakeholders, you will find showing them what you have done easier than ever before. This chapter discusses various types of measurement schemes and provides six keys to making measurement work. It also presents a balanced scorecard approach to reporting your accomplishments.

Measuring Intangibles

What you provide through your corporate university ultimately affects your organization's bottom line. The effect of what you do is felt in many ways, from the actual skills the corporate university provides employees to its collaboration and knowledge sharing activities and the forum it creates to enhance communication. For some, the impact will be evident and no further proof of your success will be needed. But most corporate universities will be asked to show how they have created an impact. You will be called on to demonstrate how all of your work contributes to the organization's success. Your challenge will be to find measurements and metrics that can convey this impact in a credible manner.

This is a very different way of approaching metrics for training and education compared to the old mindset. Historically, the focus of corporate education has been on the individual. For the new corporate university, the focus is on the organization. You will need to measure not how much an individual learns from the courses you provide but how much the organization has gained as a result.

Six Keys to Making Measurement Work

There are six simple, but often overlooked, criteria that have to be in place before any set of measures makes sense or is credible to the organization.

1. *Know who cares about the measures.* Identify the stakeholders and make sure the measures are reporting data and information that give them

a sense of how well you are moving toward their goals. There are at least four sets of stakeholders all expecting different things from the corporate university. There is management and the management team, the employees in general, the students and participants in the learning, and vendors of training products and services. Each group of stakeholders also expects to receive different benefits from the corporate university. You and your governance committee will have to decide which of these stakeholders is primary and what expectations you can fulfill and measure in a credible way.

Table 10.1 shows these various stakeholders and briefly summarizes some of the things they give and expect from the corporate university. You should spend some time with the governance committee and review these. Remove any that do not seem to fit your situation and add others that are not included here.

TABLE 10.1
Stakeholder Contributions and Expectations

Stakeholder	What They Contribute	What They Expect
Management	Budget	Highly effective development
	Support	Appropriate development to meet corporate goals
	Insight into strategic direction	
Employees	Their skills and competencies	Appropriate development to retain and excel at their job
	Their knowledge	Clear understanding of what is available, when, to whom
	Insight into emerging issues	
Students	Their time	High-quality development
	Their previous experiences and knowledge	Solid feedback
		Ongoing coaching
Vendors	Their expertise and skills	A long-term relationship
	Their content knowledge	Honest feedback on quality of product or service
	Flexibility in customizing and negotiating	Accurate administration
	Positive interactions	Prompt payment

2. *Set all the measures in a context.* This simply means providing appropriate metrics by being aware of the issues and the concerns of the key stakeholders. If the organization is going through a transformation process, the appropriate metrics are very different from those that you would focus on when times are stable and you are pursuing more routine development. Context is also about framing the numbers so that they answer useful questions. For example, a useful question could be whether or not the organization is developing people fast enough to meet the needs of managers. The answer can be framed as how the corporate university responded and how quickly people were able to do the expected work compared to a standard or an expectation that the corporate university had negotiated with the managers. Context means numbers do not exist without expectations.

3. *Embrace simplicity.* Keep the metrics simple and few. No one wants to look at ten or fifteen different metrics—especially when they are presented in ten-point type on a PowerPoint slide. Make sure the metrics you choose are based on common sense and contain no assumptions that you have not discussed with your stakeholders. For example, we saw a set of metrics rolled out based on the assumption that the stakeholders were focused on cost. There were numerous measures showing how inexpensive the training was compared to other providers and how efficiently they were delivering the courses. The stakeholders, in this case, felt that inexpensive meant low quality. They were much more interested in quality and results, but were bombarded with cost data. The corporate university lost credibility and had to do months of damage control.

4. *Create and get agreement on a set of standards.* Working with a subcommittee of your governance committee, engage in a discussion about what excellent performance would look like for the corporate university. Define base expectations and levels of performance that you will adhere to and try to exceed. For example, the expectation of the stakeholders might be that all managers have employees with skills and competencies that make them eligible for more advanced jobs. The standard might be that 80 percent of employees working for any given manager will be able to move into a promotional position without additional development. Standards are benchmarks of excellence.

5. *Be sure all your measures answer useful questions.* One way to set up an initial group of measures is to work with your subcommittee to build a list of questions that they would like to see answered each month, quarter, or year. For example, how quickly do new employees become productive? Is this improving? You can also include questions that might focus on the impact of an individual class. For example, do the managers who partici-

pated in the "Managing Performance" class have less employee turnover than those who did not participate? The answers to this list of questions will be the measures that make the most sense to the governance committee. Another way to do this is to reverse the process and list some possible metrics. Then try to write the question that the measure is the answer to. Either way works, but in the end you will have a very well-thought-out scorecard.

A common metric that stakeholders ask for is number of people who have completed a particular curriculum. This is an easy metric to gather, but it really tells the stakeholders nothing. Encourage those who pose the questions to strive for meaningful ones that will more closely give a picture of your contribution—not your activity.

Exercise 10.1 is useful to start a discussion about metrics.

EXERCISE 10.1

Measuring Success

Before going further into methodologies, please take a moment to answer the question: How does your organization's leadership measure success in general (that is, how does an individual worker, a business unit, or the finance office know they have had a successful year)?

_____

_____

_____

_____

_____

_____

_____

_____

_____

_____

_____

_____

_____

6. *Be sure you have control over the outcome of the metric.* We see many organizations reporting out figures over which they have very little or no control. For example, at a very basic level, attendance is not something you have control over. If an employee doesn't show up, that is not your fault. That is, unless your delivery methods are so bad that no one wants to endure them. If the metric you are reporting is controlled by outside influence—other people or events—it will not be a real measure of what the corporate university contributes.

Kirkpatrick's Four Levels

Most of you are probably familiar with Kirkpatrick's (1994) four-level model of training and development performance. These levels are a useful way to think about measuring what you do, but you will need to move into Level 4 if you want measures that will resonate with senior management.

The levels are briefly summarized with comments below.

Level 1: Reaction

This is the level of measurement most organizations use if they use anything at all. It is characterized by forms that are given to students at the end of classes to get their reaction to the material and instructor. Although it is useful to gather this information to improve the delivery or refine an instructor's skills, it does not answer any important questions about performance. A way to slightly improve the impact of these sheets is to engage the learners sooner in the evaluation process—even before the class starts.

The evaluation sheets can be handed out ahead of the work so that participants will understand that they are evaluating. You can include traditional questions about the program and instructor, but also include questions such as (1) Did I get full value from this course? (2) Were there preparations I could have made to make this course more meaningful? (3) Are there ways I could have engaged with the material or leader more effectively to personalize the information for my work?

Level 2: Learning

This level tests mastery of content. All of us are familiar with this level because it is the only one used in schools and universities. However, once we get into some type of organization, we no longer typically test people. A way to do this is to give a pre- and posttest to see what the level of mastery was prior to the class and again at the completion. For example, the pretest can ask the participant how he or she handles a particular challenge (addressed by the course) in his or her work today. The posttest can ask the participant how he or she will handle the challenge in the future. Almost all computer-based training and Internet training includes Level 2 evaluation built into their programs.

Emphasis should be placed on personal interpretation of the learning and specific action steps the participant plans to take. The posttest can also ask participants what they believe will be necessary to support their continued learning curve in a particular area: What database, coaching, or future course work might be helpful to them?

Level 3: Application

This level attempts to determine whether participants are able to actually perform the skills learned or incorporate the ideas that were taught into their daily work. In the corporate university, Level 3 is key. Course participants should understand early and often that their success on the job is the ultimate measurement of their successful learning experience. Again, the focus must be on the individual's application of what was learned to the work, not on the course itself. Because the corporate university is closely aligned to business goals and organizational strategies, implementing the skills and concepts the participants acquired should be expected.

The corporate university should have feedback systems in place so that participants' managers, coworkers, and even customers can have some input into an ongoing evaluation of how the course affected their job. Level 3 is tied to Level 2 evaluation because participants will identify from the beginning what specific learning they are seeking and how they want that learning to contribute to the organization. Level 3 measurements will be pivotal to your success in using metrics to demonstrate the corporate university's value. Participants, their coworkers, and managers will all contribute to your database about how much learning and improvement occurred through the corporate university.

Level 4: Return on Investment

At this level, you are showing in a qualitative or quantitative manner the real value the corporate university has had on the organization. This is where you gather actual dollars-and-cents proof that your corporate university is worth the organization's investment of time and commitment.

To develop effective Level 4 metrics, you will have to work with the finance people and with management to gather before-and-after business data in the area where the corporate university is providing training and education. By showing that you improved efficiency, reduced mistakes, or contributed to greater sales, you show the value of the corporate university. For example, the key measure for sales people might be the percentage of closed deals per sales person. The Level 4 evaluation would gather such data before and after a learning event or process (being careful to discount any intervening events, such as the introduction of a new wonder product).

Participants, their teams, and managers can all be involved in identifying the key pointers to success—the results being sought and the specific outcomes that prove or disprove effectiveness of a particular course.

Efficiency and Effectiveness

There are two sides to consider when talking about metrics. On the one hand, there are numbers and measures that report activity and efficiency. These are figures that report on costs, speed, numbers of attendees, number of programs, and so forth. It is always useful to have a gauge of efficiency, and these measures are most easily benchmarked or compared to other organizations. However, they are also the least strategic and have the least impact on the organization. They are useful for your own purposes to make sure you are keeping costs at reasonable levels and that you are delivering the content in a way that is consistent with other organizations.

On the other hand, there are measures of effectiveness that are far more powerful. These are measures of more complex and more strategic factors. These measures tell the stakeholders how well new hires are performing, how thoroughly managers are using the concepts they have been taught, and whether or not there are enough employees ready with the skills needed for a particular project. All the metrics you report should strike a balance between these.

The Scorecard Concept

Increasingly, corporate universities are using a scorecard concept to report their accomplishments and show the balance between the two. Table 10.2 illustrates this concept.

TABLE 10.2

Stakeholders and What They Might Expect to Learn from Metrics

Management	Students
Efficiency	**Efficiency**
Cost	Cost of classes
Speed of development	Length of training
Effectiveness	**Effectiveness**
Time to productivity of new hires	Skills acquired
Reduction in manufacturing errors	Time invested versus amount learned
	Satisfaction with instruction
Vendors	**Employees**
Efficiency	**Efficiency**
Speed of decisions	Speed to gain new skills
Length of contracts	Number who can receive training
Time needed to develop classes	**Effectiveness**
Effectiveness	Time required to gain skills
Quality of their instruction	Expertise of employees returning from training
Depth of content	

Emphasizing Metrics

As metrics are central to your corporate university, it will be helpful to have materials that clearly communicate how measurement can be incorporated into all the activities of the corporate university. Your evaluation forms and tests should communicate to employees that knowledge learned is more important than learning activity. You can find ways to emphasize the importance of metrics to your organization's leadership and employees by letting them know that you are concerned with the application of knowledge and the bottom-line results of learning. For example, one organization that does Level 2 testing on all their courses takes a hard line: if a person does not achieve an 80 percent or above on the posttest, the employee does not get credit for the course. But it is also important to measure the qualitative side of learning and get opinions and feedback on the value of the learning experience from those who learned, as well as from managers.

How to Use the Data

Our experience has been that the metrics must be developed into a usable report and delivered to the right people before the metrics have value.

In one corporate university, each program manager compiled quarterly reports for the departments under his or her responsibility. The program manager presented the results in a staff meeting so that there were opportunities to explore the results and answer questions. The first time managers received this information they were surprised. The efficiency data showed that at least one-third of their training dollars was going to late cancellations and to pay for employees who did not show up for the classes—a very poor use of training money. The managers then took action to see that employees who signed up for learning actually attended and completed the learning event.

Yearly metrics for the entire organization should be presented and reviewed with senior management and the governance board. The governance board may want to see metrics quarterly.

Action Steps

You can use the list of questions in Exercise 10.2 on page 117 to jump-start conversations with your governance board, staff, and key executives in your organization about how metrics will be incorporated into the organization. Answer the questions in Exercise 10.2, and use Template 10.1 during face-to-face meetings about metrics (and subsequently to share your policies about metrics).

Conclusion

Most companies suffer from not keeping and using metrics. The corporate university and management then make decisions without adequate information. However, a few organizations make the other mistake and collect too many data. Unnecessary measurement takes up resources and the data aren't used. The best approach is to collect only the data that are useful to your management and corporate university for decision making. We also find it wise to focus on building Level 2 and Level 3 evaluation into learning events or processes. Learning and improved performance are what matter most.

In some organizations what matters more than metrics are the positive comments senior management hears about the corporate university. If they intuitively feel that the corporate university is adding value and have some solid examples of success, they will be less concerned with the details of metrics. Metrics can be discounted if senior management doesn't hear or experience positive feedback about the corporate university's programs.

EXERCISE 10.2

Metrics Planning

How much money and time are the governance board willing to spend on metrics?

_____
_____
_____

What metrics are important to them?

_____
_____
_____
_____
_____

How do they define success?

_____
_____
_____
_____
_____

How often will data be gathered?

_____
_____
_____
_____
_____

Will metrics be tracked on all learning events or only on selected events?

_____
_____
_____

TEMPLATE 10.1

Stakeholders

Stakeholders

Management

What Does Management Want?

What Do Learners Contribute?

Learners

What Do Learners Want?

What Do Employees Contribute?

What Does Management Contribute?

Corporate University

Employees

Vendors

What Do Vendors Want?

What Do Vendors Contribute?

What Do Employees Want?

Designed by Eileen Clegg

Chapter 11
Final Thoughts

AFTER HAVING WORKED your way through this book, you should now have planned a corporate university equipped to help employees acquire the skills and knowledge they need to contribute to business results. This is the ultimate goal of any corporate university, and how well you are perceived to have provided the right framework and content for employee effectiveness will determine your success.

The key lesson of enduring and successful corporate universities, such as Motorola's, McDonald's, and General Electric's, is their ability to continuously adapt to new circumstances and needs. The strategic direction you chose back in Chapter Two is likely to evolve over time, and even the stakeholders may change as your organization chooses new leaders and moves into new markets.

But the curriculums you put in place and the methods you use to involve employees in learning are the most volatile. A curriculum needs to change quickly to meet emerging needs and must support people at various stages of need. This means how you encourage and organize informal, as well as formal, learning will be important. Your ability to attract resources and focus learning where it is most needed will be tests of your leadership and a sign of how highly you are valued for your contribution to success. The corporate universities that have proven their ability to enable employees to meet business challenges have usually had little trouble getting the resources they need.

The Corporate Education Survey included in Chapter One of this book is a useful tool for gauging the perception that managers and employees have about the corporate university. Use this tool annually to get a formal read on how well you are seen as contributing to employee success. But even more frequently than that you should have one-on-one meetings with key managers and those within your organization who are influential. In addition, you should establish networks of employees at all levels who can give you insight and candid feedback on your effectiveness. We have worked with at least one corporate university where the staff felt they were making significant contributions and had management support, but when we conducted interviews with employees and first-level management we quickly learned that the corporate university was seen as serving only a few people—and not doing that particularly well.

It is also important to prepare a set of metrics that you will track and report to your governance committee regularly. This discipline will show whether you are moving toward your goals and help you calibrate your speed of success. These numbers will also be useful in marketing the corporate university and in creating messages that show how you have helped the organization make progress.

We have included a final template (Template 11.1) to help you bring all the elements together. We suggest that you gather all the other templates you have completed in the process of developing your corporate university and then, with your steering committee, spend several hours consolidating and refining everything onto this last template. It will serve two primary purposes. First, it will act as a catalyst to bring all your thoughts together and to see whether each of the various elements that make up the university fit together harmoniously. And second, it will become your summary communication about the corporate university. You will find it handy whenever you are asked to explain what you are doing or why you are doing it. By asking people to focus on the graphic, you move the discussion from a personal one to one about the merits of the corporate university and what it will be doing. It is an excellent way to succinctly communicate to a large number of people.

Creating and maintaining a corporate university is a process of continuous evolution, change, adaptation, and growth. A corporate university's mission and goals are always in flux, and survival usually equates to how well the leadership of the corporate university can anticipate changing needs and assist management and employees in acquiring the skills to meet those needs.

Strategic Vision

Attitude Shifts That Had to Happen:

How We Got There:

Operating Principles:

Economic Factors:

Obstacles:

Technical Issues:

How Things Were/Are:

Demographics:

Designed by Eileen Clegg

Resources

Books and Articles

Bassi, L., & McMurrer, D. (2002, March). How's your return on people? *Harvard Business Review*, p. 18.

Cairncross, F. (2002). *The company of the future.* Boston: Harvard Business School Press.

Davenport, T. O. (1999). *Human capital.* San Francisco: Jossey-Bass.

Handy, C. (1989) *The age of unreason.* Boston: Harvard Business School Press.

Handy, C. (1994). *Gods of management: The changing work of organizations.* New York: Oxford.

Hay Group. (2002, August). *Insight selections.* (http://www.haygroup.com/library/index.asp?id=166&msg=1) (Registration is required.)

Kirkpatrick, D. L. (1994). *Evaluating training programs: The four levels.* San Francisco: Berrett-Koehler.

Management student, professor and recruiter perceptions of objectives for gateway positions: An assessment. (March/April 2004). *Journal of Education for Business,* pp. 209–212.

Marquardt, M. J. (1996). *Building the learning organization.* New York: McGraw-Hill.

Meister, J. (1994). *Corporate quality universities.* New York: Irwin.

Senge, P. (1990). *The fifth discipline.* New York: Doubleday.

Zuboff, S. (1988). *In the age of the smart machine: The future of work and power.* New York: Basic Books.

Websites

Bassi Investments
(www.bassi-investments.com)

Capital Works, LLC (informal learning)
(www.capworks.com)

Global Learning Resources
(www.glresources.com)

Internet Time Group (e-learning)
(www.internettime.com)

Learnativity
(www.learnativity.com)

Ottersurf Laboratories (informal learning)
(www.ottersurf.com)

Talent Alliance
(www.talentalliance.com)

Visual Insight
(www.visualinsight.net)

Workflow Institute (technology and learning)
(www.workflowinstitute.com)

About the Authors

Kevin Wheeler is a globally known speaker, author, teacher, and consultant in human capital acquisition and development, as well as in corporate education. He has had more than twenty-five years of corporate experience in developing and managing educational programs. He is the president of Global Learning Resources, the founder and former director of National Semiconductor University, and has been responsible for the Alphatec Institute and Schwab University.

He is the author of numerous articles on human resource development, career development, recruiting, and establishing of corporate universities. He is a frequent speaker at conferences on e-learning and corporate education.

Kevin has served as adjunct faculty at San Jose State University and the University of San Francisco and on the business faculty at San Francisco State University. He has been the senior vice president for staffing and workforce development at the Charles Schwab Corporation, the vice president of human resources for Alphatec Electronics, Inc. in Thailand, and has served in a variety of human resource roles at National Semiconductor Corporation.

Eileen Clegg is a visual journalist, book author, and researcher on the future of learning. She uses visual language—a combination of words and symbols created in real time on mural-sized paper—to facilitate new perspectives and alternative mind frames in meetings and follow-up presentations. Founder of the company Visual Insight, Eileen also works with leadership groups and educators on strategic communication and innovative learning tools. She is an affiliate of Institute for the Future (www.iftf.org).

How to Use the CD-ROM

System Requirements

PC with Microsoft Windows 98SE or later
Mac with Apple OS version 8.6 or later

Using the CD With Windows

To view the items located on the CD, follow these steps:

1. Insert the CD into your computer's CD-ROM drive.

2. A window appears with the following options:

> Contents: Allows you to view the files included on the CD-ROM.
>
> Software: Allows you to install useful software from the CD-ROM.
>
> Links: Displays a hyperlinked page of websites.
>
> Author: Displays a page with information about the author(s).
>
> Contact Us: Displays a page with information on contacting the publisher or author.
>
> Help: Displays a page with information on using the CD.
>
> Exit: Closes the interface window.

If you do not have autorun enabled, or if the autorun window does not appear, follow these steps to access the CD:

1. Click Start → Run.

2. In the dialog box that appears, type d: <\\><\\> start.exe, where d is the letter of your CD-ROM drive. This brings up the autorun window described in the preceding set of steps.

3. Choose the desired option from the menu. (See Step 2 in the preceding list for a description of these options.)

In Case of Trouble

If you experience difficulty using the CD-ROM, please follow these steps:

1. Make sure your hardware and systems configurations conform to the systems requirements noted under "System Requirements" on page 127.

2. Review the installation procedure for your type of hardware and operating system. It is possible to reinstall the software if necessary.

To speak with someone in Product Technical Support, call 800-762-2974 or 317-572-3994 Monday through Friday from 8:30 A.M. to 5:00 P.M. EST. You can also contact Product Technical Support and get support information through our website at www.wiley.com/techsupport.

Before calling or writing, please have the following information available:

- Type of computer and operating system.
- Any error messages displayed.
- Complete description of the problem.

It is best if you are sitting at your computer when making the call.

Pfeiffer Publications Guide

This guide is designed to familiarize you with the various types of Pfeiffer publications. The formats section describes the various types of products that we publish; the methodologies section describes the many different ways that content might be provided within a product. We also provide a list of the topic areas in which we publish.

FORMATS

In addition to its extensive book-publishing program, Pfeiffer offers content in an array of formats, from fieldbooks for the practitioner to complete, ready-to-use training packages that support group learning.

FIELDBOOK Designed to provide information and guidance to practitioners in the midst of action. Most fieldbooks are companions to another, sometimes earlier, work, from which its ideas are derived; the fieldbook makes practical what was theoretical in the original text. Fieldbooks can certainly be read from cover to cover. More likely, though, you'll find yourself bouncing around following a particular theme, or dipping in as the mood, and the situation, dictate.

HANDBOOK A contributed volume of work on a single topic, comprising an eclectic mix of ideas, case studies, and best practices sourced by practitioners and experts in the field.

An editor or team of editors usually is appointed to seek out contributors and to evaluate content for relevance to the topic. Think of a handbook not as a ready-to-eat meal, but as a cookbook of ingredients that enables you to create the most fitting experience for the occasion.

RESOURCE Materials designed to support group learning. They come in many forms: a complete, ready-to-use exercise (such as a game); a comprehensive resource on one topic (such as conflict management) containing a variety of methods and approaches; or a collection of like-minded activities (such as icebreakers) on multiple subjects and situations.

TRAINING PACKAGE An entire, ready-to-use learning program that focuses on a particular topic or skill. All packages comprise a guide for the facilitator/trainer and a workbook for the participants. Some packages are supported with additional media—such as video—or learning aids, instruments, or other devices to help participants understand concepts or practice and develop skills.

- *Facilitator/trainer's guide* Contains an introduction to the program, advice on how to organize and facilitate the learning event, and step-by-step instructor notes. The guide also contains copies of presentation materials—handouts, presentations, and overhead designs, for example—used in the program.

- *Participant's workbook* Contains exercises and reading materials that support the learning goal and serves as a valuable reference and support guide for participants in the weeks and months that follow the learning event. Typically, each participant will require his or her own workbook.

ELECTRONIC CD-ROMs and web-based products transform static Pfeiffer content into dynamic, interactive experiences. Designed to take advantage of the searchability, automation, and ease-of-use that technology provides, our e-products bring convenience and immediate accessibility to your workspace.

METHODOLOGIES

CASE STUDY A presentation, in narrative form, of an actual event that has occurred inside an organization. Case studies are not prescriptive, nor are they used to prove a point; they are designed to develop critical analysis and decision-making skills. A case study has a specific time frame, specifies a sequence of events, is narrative in structure, and contains a plot structure—an issue (what should be/have been done?). Use case studies when the goal is to enable participants to apply previously learned theories to the circumstances in the case, decide what is pertinent, identify the real issues, decide what should have been done, and develop a plan of action.

ENERGIZER A short activity that develops readiness for the next session or learning event. Energizers are most commonly used after a break or lunch to stimulate or refocus the group. Many involve some form of physical activity, so they are a useful way to counter post-lunch lethargy. Other uses include transitioning from one topic to another, where "mental" distancing is important.

EXPERIENTIAL LEARNING ACTIVITY (ELA) A facilitator-led intervention that moves participants through the learning cycle from experience to application (also known as a Structured Experience). ELAs are carefully thought-out designs in which there is a definite learning purpose and intended outcome. Each step—everything that participants do during the activity—facilitates the accomplishment of the stated goal. Each ELA includes complete instructions for facilitating the intervention and a clear statement of goals, suggested group size and timing, materials required, an explanation of the process, and, where appropriate, possible variations to the activity. (For more detail on Experiential Learning Activities, see the Introduction to the *Reference Guide to Handbooks and Annuals*, 1999 edition, Pfeiffer, San Francisco.)

GAME A group activity that has the purpose of fostering team spirit and togetherness in addition to the achievement of a pre-stated goal. Usually contrived—undertaking a desert expedition, for example—this type of learning method offers an engaging means for participants to demonstrate and practice business and interpersonal skills. Games are effective for team building and personal development mainly because the goal is subordinate to the process—the means through which participants reach decisions, collaborate, communicate, and generate trust and understanding. Games often engage teams in "friendly" competition.

ICEBREAKER A (usually) short activity designed to help participants overcome initial anxiety in a training session and/or to acquaint the participants with one another. An icebreaker can be a fun activity or can be tied to specific topics or training goals. While a useful tool in itself, the icebreaker comes into its own in situations where tension or resistance exists within a group.

INSTRUMENT A device used to assess, appraise, evaluate, describe, classify, and summarize various aspects of human behavior. The term used to describe an instrument depends primarily on its format and purpose. These terms include survey, questionnaire, inventory, diagnostic, survey, and poll. Some uses of instruments include providing instrumental feedback to group members, studying here-and-now processes or functioning within a group, manipulating group composition, and evaluating outcomes of training and other interventions.

Instruments are popular in the training and HR field because, in general, more growth can occur if an individual is provided with a method for focusing specifically on his or her own behavior. Instruments also are used to obtain information that will serve as a basis for change and to assist in workforce planning efforts.

Paper-and-pencil tests still dominate the instrument landscape with a typical package comprising a facilitator's guide, which offers advice on administering the instrument and interpreting the collected data, and an initial set of instruments. Additional instruments are available separately. Pfeiffer, though, is investing heavily in e-instruments. Electronic instrumentation provides effortless distribution and, for larger groups particularly, offers advantages over paper-and-pencil tests in the time it takes to analyze data and provide feedback.

LECTURETTE A short talk that provides an explanation of a principle, model, or process that is pertinent to the participants' current learning needs. A lecturette is intended to establish a common language bond between the trainer and the participants by providing a mutual frame of reference. Use a lecturette as an introduction to a group activity or event, as an interjection during an event, or as a handout.

MODEL A graphic depiction of a system or process and the relationship among its elements. Models provide a frame of reference and something more tangible, and more easily remembered, than a verbal explanation. They also give participants something to "go on," enabling them to track their own progress as they experience the dynamics, processes, and relationships being depicted in the model.

ROLE PLAY A technique in which people assume a role in a situation/scenario: a customer service rep in an angry-customer exchange, for example. The way in which the role is approached is then discussed and feedback is offered. The role play is often repeated using a different approach and/or incorporating changes made based on feedback received. In other words, role playing is a spontaneous interaction involving realistic behavior under artificial (and safe) conditions.

SIMULATION A methodology for understanding the interrelationships among components of a system or process. Simulations differ from games in that they test or use a model that depicts or mirrors some aspect of reality in form, if not necessarily in content. Learning occurs by studying the effects of change on one or more factors of the model. Simulations are commonly used to test hypotheses about what happens in a system—often referred to as "what if?" analysis—or to examine best-case/worst-case scenarios.

THEORY A presentation of an idea from a conjectural perspective. Theories are useful because they encourage us to examine behavior and phenomena through a different lens.

TOPICS

The twin goals of providing effective and practical solutions for workforce training and organization development and meeting the educational needs of training and human resource professionals shape Pfeiffer's publishing program. Core topics include the following:

Leadership & Management

Communication & Presentation

Coaching & Mentoring

Training & Development

E-Learning

Teams & Collaboration

OD & Strategic Planning

Human Resources

Consulting

What will you find on pfeiffer.com?

• The best in workplace performance solutions for training and HR professionals

• Downloadable training tools, exercises, and content

• Web-exclusive offers

• Training tips, articles, and news

• Seamless on-line ordering

• Author guidelines, information on becoming a Pfeiffer Affiliate, and much more

Discover more at www.pfeiffer.com

Customer Care

Have a question, comment, or suggestion? Contact us! We value your feedback and we want to hear from you.

For questions about this or other Pfeiffer products, you may contact us by:

E-mail: **customer@wiley.com**

Mail: **Customer Care Wiley/Pfeiffer**
10475 Crosspoint Blvd.
Indianapolis, IN 46256

Phone: **(US) 800-274-4434** (Outside the US: 317-572-3985)

Fax: **(US) 800-569-0443** (Outside the US: 317-572-4002)

To order additional copies of this title or to browse other Pfeiffer products, visit us online at **www.pfeiffer.com**.

For **Technical Support** questions call **(800) 274-4434.**

For authors guidelines, log on to www.pfeiffer.com and click on "Resources for Authors."

If you are . . .

A **college bookstore, a professor, an instructor, or work in higher education** and you'd like to place an order or request an exam copy, please contact jbreview@wiley.com.

A **general retail bookseller** and you'd like to establish an account or speak to a local sales representative, contact Melissa Grecco at 201-748-6267 or mgrecco@wiley.com.

An **exclusively on-line bookseller**, contact Amy Blanchard at 530-756-9456 or ablanchard @wiley.com or Jennifer Johnson at 206-568-3883 or jjohnson@wiley.com, both of our Online Sales department.

A **librarian or library representative**, contact John Chambers in our Library Sales department at 201-748-6291 or jchamber@wiley.com.

A **reseller, training company/consultant, or corporate trainer**, contact Charles Regan in our Special Sales department at 201-748-6553 or cregan@wiley.com.

A **specialty retail distributor** (includes specialty gift stores, museum shops, and corporate bulk sales), contact Kim Hendrickson in our Special Sales department at 201-748-6037 or khendric@wiley.com.

Purchasing for the **Federal government**, contact Ron Cunningham in our Special Sales department at 317-572-3053 or rcunning@wiley.com.

Purchasing for a **State or Local government**, contact Charles Regan in our Special Sales department at 201-748-6553 or cregan@wiley.com.